PREPARATION FOR CRITERION-REFERENCED TESTS:

A BRIEF REVIEW OF SCIENTIFIC COMPETENCIES

FOR

TEACHERS OF MIDDLE GRADES

MARY OELLERICH DALNOKI MIKLOS

GEORGIA SOUTHWESTERN COLLEGE

Dedicated to my Father, Charles Grover Oellerich, the greatest gentleman I have ever known, whose devotion to his family made possible this manuscript.

iii

COMMON LABORATORY EQUIPMENT

GRADUATED CYLINDER

ROUND BOTTOM FLASK

FLAT BOTTOM FLASK

ERLENMEYER FLASK

BEAKER

TEST TUBE

THISTLE TUBE

TEST TUBE BRUSH

PLAIN MICROSCOPE SLIDE

SQUARE & ROUND COVER GLASS

WATCH GLASS

FROSTED END MICROSCOPE SLIDE

PETRI DISH

PORCELAIN EVAPORATING DISH

TEST TUBE CLAMP (METAL)

PIPE-STEM TRIANGLE

WIRE GAUZE (ASBESTOS CENTER)

ACKNOWLEDGEMENTS

To the requirement of some state departments of education that teachers meet certain minimum standards of competency before being eligible for the professional teacher's certificate, this book, owes its existence.

To my students over a period of thirty-four years I owe the motivation and inspiration necessary for the development of the manuscript.

To my college students, prospective teachers, over a period of twenty years I owe their many suggestions, ideas, and contributions.

To the many students I have taught in elementary, junior high, senior high, and college I am deeply grateful for the opportunity to follow and to succeed in my chosen profession.

The imperfections in this book are the author's responsibility.

COMMON LABORATORY EQUIPMENT

BURET CLAMP

SPRING
TUBING CLAMP

RING STAND
AND RINGS

RIGHT ANGLE
CLAMP

SCREW
TUBING CLAMP

FORCEPS

TONGS

TIN SNIPS

SPATULA

GOOSENECK
LAMP

SPRING
BALANCE

TABLE OF CONTENTS

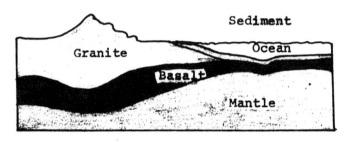

The basic difference between the continents and
the ocean basins is that they are made of
different crustal materials. The continents
are underlaid by granite, floating on heavier
basalt; the oceans lie on basalt. This
digrammatic cross-section shows the difference
at the edge of a continent.

A BRIEF REVIEW OF SCIENTIFIC COMPETENCIES
FOR
TEACHERS OF MIDDLE GRADES

The boards of education of some states have
formulated plans for assuring the educational
personnel certified possess the competencies-
knowledge, skills, and attitudes-necessary to
facilitate desired student learning. It was
decided that this could be done most effectively
by making fundamental changes in the current
preparation and certification process.

One of the changes is to separate, in part,
the certification and preparation functions by
introducing job-related certification measures
that are external to institutional grades,
courses and approved programs. Teaching field
criterion-referenced tests are to be used to
determine whether prospective teachers possess
essential content knowledge in their teaching
field. Tests given to middle grades teachers
usually cover the following areas: mathematics,
science, social studies, and language arts.

This book is developed to serve as a review
of the scientific competencies required of middle
grades teachers and not initial learning thereof.
Contained herein are the teaching field objectives
all of which have been vertified as important
content requirements for middle grades teachers.
If the state in which you teach or will teach
requires you to take a criterion-referenced test
not all of the objectives in this book will have
had test items written for them. All objectives
are requirements for middle grades teachers and
a sampling on them will be tested.

The purpose of this book is to explicitly
review knowledge needed by middle grades teachers.
Further, this review should assist in preparing
for the criterion-referenced content knowledge
test. Prospective middle grades teachers are

encouraged to study these materials, which will enhance their understanding of the science content field and alleviate any unnecessary concerns about the nature of the criterion-referenced tests.

Since this book is developed to serve as a review and not initial learning, a student might need further information on a particular competency for complete mastery. In such cases the student is urged to seek other sources and record important notes as needed.

College instructors teaching the method courses for middle grades teachers may wish to use this book to review basic competencies with their students. This book can be used as a supplementary aid with any textbook.

Students may want to review the basic competencies on their own without any guidance since the book is constructed in such a manner that this can be done.

Along with this review go hopes for a rewarding teaching career.

Dr. Mary Oellerich Dalnoki Miklos
Professor of Mathematics and Science
    Education
Georgia Southwestern College
Americus Georgia

COMMON LABORATORY EQUIPMENT

FUNNEL

TRIPOD

CRUCIBLE
AND COVER

ROUND FILE

1-HOLE
RUBBER STOPPER

TRIANGULAR FILE

2-HOLE
RUBBER STOPPER

FLAT FILE

ELECTRIC
KNIFE SWITCH

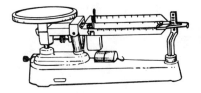

TRIPLE-BEAM BALANCE

COMMON LABORATORY EQUIPMENT

ELECTRIC LIGHT
RECEPTACLE

LIQUEFIED PETROLEUM
GAS (PROPANE) BURNER

ALCOHOL
LAMP

BURNER
WING TOP

BUNSEN
BURNER

TEST TUBE
CLAMP (WOOD)

TEST TUBE
RACK

DRY CELL
NO. 6

A BRIEF REVIEW OF SCIENTIFIC COMPETENCIES
FOR
TEACHERS OF MIDDLE GRADES

Competency 1: Evaluate the accuracy of scientific information through the use of appropriate resources and experimentation.

A fundamental method of collecting scientific data and information is simply the use of the senses to discover what is happening. Yet, real observation requires thoughtful looking. It is closely linked with being able to describe what is observed.

Observation may be purely visual in nature, or achieved with the aid of suitable instruments. Microscopes reveal the tiny bacteria, viruses, and other small organisms. Telescopes bring distant galaxies and other celestial bodies into view. Radio receivers change the radio waves into audible sound waves. These are but a few of the remarkable devises that man has invented to increase and extend the powers of his sense organs.

Another method of collecting data is measurement. Measurement involves the use of devices which allows the substitution of objective numbers for subjective observations. The human senses can be fooled into giving inaccurate and distorted impressions. Measurement can make observations accurate and objective. Since accurate observation is an absolute must in science, measuring devices are basic tools of the researcher. The simplest measuring devices include rulers for distance, scales for weight, thermometers for temperature, manometers for pressure, voltmeters and anmeters for electricity.

A method of combining observation and measurement to find new data is experimentation. experimentation differs from simple or mere observation in that it involves a deliberate disturbance of the "normal" course of events. Experiments may be performed in order to recheck generally accepted facts. Also, experiments may be performed to discover laws governing certain events or conditions. Most importantly, experiments may be preformed to test newly conceived hypotheses.

Observation, measurement, and experimentation are the first steps in scientific investigation. They are the data producing procedures and are the spring boards for future ideas and hypotheses.

Quantifiable data amounts to description by the use of numbers. These numbers are obtained by making measurements. The methods of measurement vary according to the nature of the experiment. Instruments are often used to aid in making the measurements, since they are better adapted to help gather facts than the unaided senses. You may choose to weigh something on a scale, time something with a watch, measure something with a ruler, or simply count some results. The numbers obtained by measurement often reveal various laws of nature.

To see the advantages of collecting quanifiable data consider the astronomer trying to describe the sun and the moon. He can say the sun is much, much bigger than the moon. Or he can say the diameter of the sun is about 860,000 miles. The diameter of the moon is about 2,000 miles. The comparison using numbers based upon measurement provides more understanding.

In the elementary school most science has been mainly qualitative. Children should use quantitative methods as well. In this way, they will gain a better understanding of the subject and also get practice in the skill of making measurements.

Consider an experiment on plant growth. Two potted plants of the same type and size are obtained. One is put in a window and the other is placed in a closet. The results can easily be seen by simple observation only, but the student's understanding and skills will be increased by allowing them to weigh and measure the plants.

Test your knowledge of competency 1.

1. Quantifiable data amounts to description by the use of
    a. intuition
    b. numbers
    c. opinion
    d. judgement

2. Which of the following is not a quantitative method?
    a. weighing
    b. measuring
    c. touching
    d. timing

3. A method of obtaining data by use of the sense organs is
    a. testing
    b. experimentation
    c. observation
    d. inovation

4. Collecting data by changing the "normal" events of nature is
    a. experimentation
    b. thinking
    c. measurement
    d. devices

Answers: 1. b, 2. c, 3. c, 4. a

Competency 2: Organize given items of scientific information by selecting correct lables, names, codes, recording processes, classifications, and categories.

When research data have been collected, and before they can be analyzed, they must be assembled and organized. The purpose of organizing data is to speed up the process of analysis. Data that are collected can be expressed in two ways, qualitatively and quanitatively.

There are no rigid rules that apply to the way data in qualitative form should be organized. Organization of nonnumerical material is a matter of accomplishing the objective of research - solving a problem. If there is any generalization that can be made, it is that data should be examined for patterns of order in the data itself or for similarities to other situations in which order has been perceived previously: patterns, relationship or order.

Whereas, the organization of data in qualitative form may be described only in generalities, numerical data are subject to the processes of mathematical analysis. So, organization of material expressed quantitatively is a matter of preparing the data in ways that are known to expose mathematical patterns and order whenever they exist.

Quantitative data lend themselves to mathematical and scientific analysis. Before mathematical tools can be applied, however, it is necessary to organize quantitative data. Organi-

4

zation of data (1) helps insure that patterns stand out, and (2) gives the researcher a basis for the selection of proper analytical tools.

Data analysis always implies the organizing and summarizing of observations. Perhaps the most familiar way of doing this is through classification: the process of setting up boxes, categories, or types, into which individual observations can be placed.

Classification is important for both the conception and analysis stages of the research. Once we have established our categories, observations then fall conveniently into place.

Frequency distribution is a special kind of classification system used very commonly. Frequency refers to the number of times a given observation or class of observations occur. Like any other classification system, frequency distributions reveal patterns in data by summarizing or grouping observations.

After the goal has been identified and the data has been gathered and prepared, the final problem to consider is how the data should be organized for presentation to the students. This problem of how much the data should be organized does not have any clear-cut answers. With each lesson several factors must be weighed by the teacher: the amount of available time for a lesson, the student's ability level, the relative importance of process and content goals, and the importance of communicating an accurate view of the nature of science. The amount of structure the teacher imposes upon the data will vary as these goals are given different priorities.

A teacher may want to be very structured and give explicit directions to the students about how to interact with the data. Or, he may want to use an alternative procedure such as giving the students the materials and allowing them to achieve a certain goal.

When data is more organized than necessary, it gives the students an inaccurate view of what science is really all about. Scientists usually work with unorganized and unprocessed data. One of the first task for a scientist is to try and find some pattern or trend so that concept formulations and generalizations can begin. Students are given a false view of science and the activities of scientists when the organization of data is all done for them.

Data that is overorganized does not give students the opportunity to experiment with the data to make sense out of it. It deprives students of the chance to practice their skills of working data into a particular pattern. To summarize, the degree of organization of data prior to the lesson depends mainly on your judgement, as do many decisions in teaching.

When students are ready to compare the data to the hypothesis, the next step in an inquiry activity will take place. While comparing the data to the hypothesis, the students will be able to determine if the hypothesis can be accepted or needs to be rejected. In order to make adequate comparisons, the data must be organized in some way, especially if there are large amounts of information or the data gathering took a long time.

Two ways to order the data are to graph it or to chart it. Helping the class to graph the data provides wonderful opportunities to teach students a new skill - how to construct and read graphs. As you are graphing data with students, you should follow several points. The independent variable is generally placed on the horizontal axis and the dependent variable on the vertical axis. The graph should be clearly labeled so that a reader can tell from the title what is being described. Charts allow easy comparisons between different values of the indepentent variable.

Science in the elementary school has been primarily qualitative in nature; very little has been quantitative. Quantitative results should also be stressed. The children are constantly exposed to the "why" and "what" of science and rarely to the "how much". As a result, a great opportunity is being missed not only to show the child key relationships, but also to provide for practice in measurement, which is one of the key operations of science and the scientist.

Test your knowledge of competency 2.

1. Data that are collected can be expressed in two ways
    a. numerically and nonnumerically
    b. regularly and irregularly
    c. qualitatively and quantitatively
    d. none of the above

2. Organization of data
    a. helps insure that patterns stand out
    b. is the first step in the scientific process
    c. gives the researcher a basis for the selection of proper tools
    d. both a and b
    e. both a and c

3. The independent variable is generally placed on
    a. the vertical axis
    b. the horizonal axis
    c. either one
    d. neither one

Answers: 1. c, 2. e 3. b

Competency 3: Evaluate the use of the scientific method as a problem-solving technique, and/or indicate valid instances of its use.

There are six distinguishing features of scientific thinking:

1. science is based on facts
2. science employs the principles of analysis as a fundamental procedure in the comprehension of complex phenomena
3. science employs hypotheses in the thinking involved
4. scientific thinking is characterized by freedom from emotional bias
5. science utilizes accurate measurement
6. science employs quantitative methods in the treatment of its data.

Sources of authority found in our nation are scholars, philosophers, and scientists. The worthwhileness of their counsel depends upon their judgement, intelligence, and scholarship. From the dawn of civilization man has appealed to his oracles, his intellectual superiors, his church, his state, his king, and to his God or gods for guidance.

Although man does appeal to custom, tradition, and authority in his attempts to derive satisfactory solutions to perplexing problems, no single source of evidence is more universally employed in the search for truth than is personal experience. This source of evidence provides knowledge of most ordinary affairs in everyday life.

We gather information through the process of observation. A child goes beyond these immediate observations to construct patterns to predict future observations and explain the events that were observed. The extensions and interpretations of these observations are concerned with inferences, associations, comparisons and predictions. Through these processes, much of our understanding of the world is accomplished. The elementary science teacher plays a vital role in the process be selecting important science concepts and generalizations to teach.

The ability of the child to make associations or inferences based upon observations, include more classifying, summarizing, and predicting to explain certain events. It is important for a child to decide the validity of these interpretations. This is essentially a thinking skill.

The student may need to be reminded that a scientist makes all his observations first, then he interprets them. The students are simply to record what they see--for example concerning the growth of plants. After they have completed all their observations, they interpret them to accept or reject the hypotesis or prediction as to "what do you think will happen if ...?"

If students work in groups or individually, the class as a whole may make the interpretations.

First, the students select and establish the problem.

Second, they would formulate the hypothesis.

Third, structure the test for the inferences. These include making operational definitions, controlling variables, organizing experiments and recording the interpretation of data. The children should receive a great deal of direction from the teacher. As pupils gain more experience in interpreting specific data and the experimentation process they should receive less help.

9

In predicting a student must be able to make reasonable predictions on the basis of available data. This is an inferring skill.

As predicting is employed in the elementary science, it implies forecasting some future event from a solid base of evidence. For example: After graphing experimental data and finding that it takes three metal washers to counterbalance one marble on different sides of the scales, and nine washers to counterbalance three marbles; a student can predict that six washers will counterbalance two marbles and twelve washers will counterbalance four marbles.

Inquiry lessons that require students to make these predictions, associations and comparisons, and test these by experimentations will help to develop the process skills.

The following is an example of a lesson for a teacher in a fourth grade classroom. The lesson is on "Heat and the States of Matter". There are three subconcepts to be taught.
1. Many different substances will change their form with the addition of heat.
2. Energy is required to change the state of matter.
3. Molecules of warm liquids move faster than molecules of cold liquids.

To achieve the first concept a teacher may place some beewax, some ice and some solder (tin or lead) on a tin plate and heat the plate over a propane torch. Questions to ask: What did you see? What can we conclude? If the teacher knows how to ask opening questions along with selected reinforcement the children will conclude that things change states when they are heated, only the temperature at which it happens is different. This exercise is an inquiry demonstration which involves the skills of observing and inferring.

In the second concept the teacher could use

a time temperature graph. This would show when
ice cubes are placed in a beaker and heated the
temperature will rise rapidly to 0 degrees and
remain there for a time before rising again. This
is to show that ice absorbs energy as it changes to
water. This activity develops the skill of interpretation of data.

In the third concept a student is given two
bottles, one containing hot water and the other
cold. One drop of food coloring is added to each.
The students make observations and inferences about
what they see.

Test your knowlegde of competency 3.

1. Science is mainly based on
    a. facts
    b. theory
    c. experiments
    d. hypotheses

2. Who provides the sources for scientific research?
    a. scholars
    b. philosophers
    c. scientists
    d. a, b, and c
    e. a and b

3. The extensions and interpretations of observations include
    a. investigating, characterizing, and
       describing
    b. associations, comparisons, and predictions
    c. modeling, symbols, changes
    d. description

4. As predicting is employed in the elementary
   school science it implies
    a. stating problems
    b. describing events
    c. forecasting future events
    d. stating facts
Answers: 1. a 2. d 3. b 4. c

Competency 4-1: Describe the general structure and function of plant and animal cells.

Introduction

Almost all living things are made of cells. Some tiny forms of life consist of only one cell. Larger forms of life consist of many cells. That is why cells are called the basic unit of life.

The human body is made up of billions upon billions of cells. They are so tiny they can only be seen with the aid of a microscope.

The smallest cells are bacteria. These one-celled forms of life can barely be seen with a microscope. Nerve cells are the largest cells. Some of them are more than three feet long.

Cells consist of three main parts: the cell membrane, the cytoplasm, and the nucleus.

There are many kinds of cells and each cell does a special job. One of the most remarkable cell activity is cell division. Most kinds of cells divide into two new cells. Both the new cells are exactly like the original cell.

Plants and animals grow because of cell division. New cells replace old or worn-out cells. As cell division slows, the body ages.

Finally, plant and animal cells differ from each other in some ways, but in a broad sense they are alike. So, we say that the cell is the unit of life.

The Main Parts of a Cell

The Cell Membrane

The cell membrane is the outermost surface of
the cell. Everything that leaves or enters the
cell must pass through it. Water, salts, oxygen,
and food must enter. Carbon dioxide, waste substances, water, and salt must also leave.

The Cytoplasm

The cytoplasm is the area where most of the
chemical work is conducted. New cell materials
are made here, and old ones are passed out.
Organic compounds from food substances are used.
They are built up into new cell structures or used
to store energy.

The substances are built into new cell substance or used as a kind of fuel. As a fuel the
supply is used for energy necessary for growth of
cell substances or activity of cell structures.
There is also a continuous outflow of final products of fuel combustion and a breakdown of worn-
out cell structures.

A cell has characteristics such as size,
shape, and a molasses-like consistency. With
cells anything that cuts off either the supply of
oxygen or the organic materials cuts off the life.

Structure of the Cytoplasm

One kind consists of minute sausage-shaped
bodies called mitochondria. They have a complex
internal structure which has been called the power-
house of the cell. Another kind of structure
consists of very extensive double membranes endoplasmic reticulum. Along the reticulum are enormous numbers of minute granules called ribosomes.
The cytoplasm also contains structures called

13

Golgi bodies. They involve the secretion of cell products.

The Cell Nucleus

The nucleus is concerned with controlling the nature of the cell. It contains threadlike material called chromatin. When a cell is about to divide this material groups together into a number of slender rods called chromosomes. The chromosomes consist of very complex chemical called nucleic acid. Known as deoxyribonucleic acid or DNA. Small bodies called nucleoli are also found in the nucleus known as ribonucleis acid or RNA.

Animal and Plant Cells

Both animal and plant cells require water and mineral salts.

Most plant cells can manufacture their own sugars and other basic substances. They do this by using the energy obtained from light together with water, carbon dioxide, and certain other raw materials--this process is known as photosynthesis.

Light is absorbed by the green pigment chlorophyll. Chlorophyll is confined in small, round, green discs called chloroplasts. There is also a large internal sac of fluid called the vacuole.

Animal cells take in water, dissolved salts, and other substances by a process of diffusion through the invisible pores of the membrane. The drinking process of cells are called pinocytosis.

14

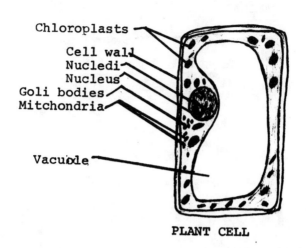

Chloroplasts

Cell wall
Nucledi
Nucleus
Goli bodies
Mitchondria

Vacuole

PLANT CELL

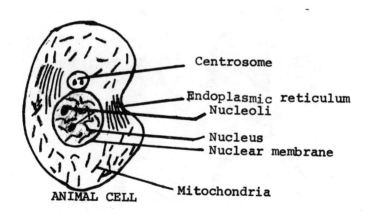

Centrosome

Endoplasmic reticulum
Nucleoli

Nucleus
Nuclear membrane

Mitochondria

ANIMAL CELL

15

ANIMAL CELL DIVIDING BY MITOSIS

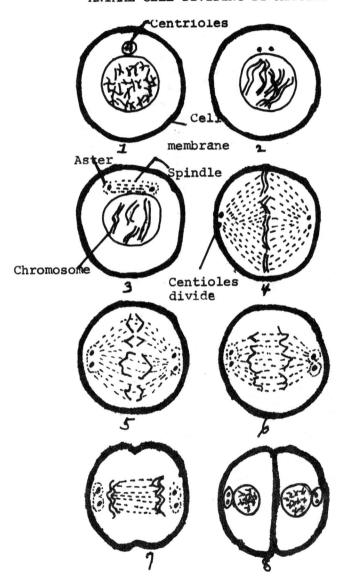

Test your knowledge of competency 4-1.

1. Cells are the basic unit of
   a. oxygen
   b. photosyntehsis
   c. life
   d. nucleus

2. Most animal and plant cells require
   a. water and minerals
   b. carbon-containing compounds
   c. oxygen
   d. a, b, and c

3. A cell is in the process of constant
   a. change
   b. division
   c. break-down
   d. diffusion

Answers: 1. c, 2. d, 3. a

Competency 4-2: Describe the general structure and function of plant and animal cells.

There is no life without cells. And just as life itself is diverse so are the forms and functions of the cells that constitute life. Some cells live alone as free-moving, independent creatures, some belong to loosely organized communities which move from place to place, and some spend their lifetime in fixed immobility as part of the tissue of a larger organism. Whatever its form, however it behaves, the cell is the basic unit of all living matter. In the cell, nature has enclosed in a microscopic package all the parts and processes necessary to the survival of life in an everchanging world.

The modern microscope has revealed an astonishing diversity in both the structure and the functions of the cell. Cells are shaped like rods, spirals, shoe boxes, spheres, daisies on the

17

stalks, snowflakes, string beans, and blobs of
jelly. In some cases, the shape of a cell is dic-
tated by its surrounding environment; this is
apparently true of the neatly shaped rectangular
cells packed in the stalk of a plant and of the
spherical floating eggs of certain marine animals.
The shape of other cells is often related to their
function. Human red-blood cells are saucer-shaped
and fairly flat, permitting the ready transfer of
the oxygen and carbon dioxide they carry throughout the body, while nerve cells have long, thin
extensions to transmit messages.

Cells can be self-sufficient generalists
capable of carrying non-independent existence;
single-celled creatures such as the ameoba and the
paramecium are examples of these free-living units.
Cells can also be specialists with a particular
job to do; these cells depend for their existence
upon a highly integrated community life with other
cells. Such cells group together to form creatures with luminous eyes on stalks, sponges that
cling to rocks, praying mantises, peacocks, tigers,
and men--the whole visible, living world around us.

For all this diversity, all cells are built
according to a fundamental design which provides
them with certain common features apparently
necessary to life. Every cell has an outer wall
which makes it a room. Within the surrounding membrane is a semifluid material called cytoplasm in
which the life activities of the cell are carried
on. At the heart of the cell is the nucleus, a
control center that bears within it the cell's
hereditary material ensuing the survival of its
line.

Cells may be classified as either plant or
animal. Plants make their own food but animals
must catch theirs. So animals move around while
plants stand still. Most plant cells have rigid
shapes while most animal cells are flexible. Flesh,
when pinched, gives and then returns to shape--a
tree does not.

There are cells that live alone and cells that live in communities. The latter can be formed into structures of amazing complexity, like the turtle, frog, flower, or a human being. The cells that go their own way remain mostly unseen blowing around in the air or slopping about for a few silent hours in the sea.

In simple terms, the plant cell can be divided into two main regions: the cell wall and the protoplast. The protoplast consists of the nucleus, the cytoplasm, which contains a variety of membrane-bound organelles, and a large vacuole containing an aqueous medium of salts and various organic molecules acting as a resevoir for the metabolic activity of the cell. However, although the great majority of plant cells conform to this general picture there is considerable variation in their size, shape, and structure and this is normally closely related to the function of the particular cell type.

Plant cells are surrounded by polysaccharide walls against which lies a thin layer of cytoplasm enclosing one or more large vacuoles. Structural rigidity is achieved by the "turgor pressure" of the cytoplasm against the cell wall. The mitotic apparatus of plant cells has a spindle, but in higher plants there are no centrioles, and cell division occurs by the growth of a new partition separating the two daughter cells. Many plant cells contain chloroplasts, which endow the cell with the important capability of converting light energy into chemical energy.

Animal cells lack a rigid cell wall surrounding thin plasma membrane. Their mitotic apparatus includes centrioles, and division occurs by constriction of the cell. They lack chloroplasts and depend ultimately on plants as their source of food and therefore of energy. Animal cells are noted for their mobility and their ability to ingest food particles that are subsequently digested inside the cell.

19

There are great differences among shapes of animal cells conditioned by their functions. The striated muscle cell is multinucleate, full of mitochondria to furnish energy necessary for the contraction of the fibrils which fill the cytoplasm. The motor neuron has long extensions of its cytoplasm, extensions sometimes meters long, which are really membrane-mediated conductors of the morphological features that make it extraordinary. The kidney cell is typified by its narrowness, in which long mitochondria lie adjacent to the cell membrane, ready to furnish the energy necessary to transport ions across that membrane. The sperm is a cell made up of a locomotory fibrillar part, surrounded by mitochondria whose task it is to move an information-loaded nucleus.

The plant and animal cell types described here are differentiated into numerous forms, each specialized for particular functions which they perform in the organism. Within a single organism like the mammalian body, one finds many different cell types such as the elongated and fibrillar striated muscle cell, the slender and branched nerve cell, the metabotically active liver cell, the osmotically active kidney cell, and the free-swimming protozoanlike sperm cell. The cells of the higher plants also vary a great deal in their structure and function. There are the undifferentiated parenchyma cells of the growing regions of the plant body, the phloem sieve tubes with their special properties for food transport, and the root hairs adapted for water and mineral absorption.

These distinct cell types represent specializations by which cells adapt to their specific roles. It is important to recognize that many specialized cell functions find their origin in general cellular phenomena occurring in attentuated form throughout the cellular world. Nerve conduction is based on action potentials that occur in all cells. Muscular contraction is based on a mechanism of conversion of chemical energy into work, which appears to occur universally, osmotic work found in a highly active form in kidney cells also appears to be a universal property of living matter.

All life on earth from the lowliest rock-bound lichen to the mightiest philosopher--exists because of a dual miracle of chemistry called photosynthesis and respiration. Through photosynthesis, a plant cell traps a tiny amount of the sun's radiant energy and uses it to convert water from the soil and carbon dioxide from the air into sugar and oxygen. Through respiration, both plant and animal cells take in oxygen and use it to turn the sugar in food into energy; the by-products of respiration, water and carbon dioxide, are returned to the atmosphere to be used once again in photosynthesis. This cycle of life is endlessly repeated. A cow eats the plants and by respiration uses the sugar's energy to produce milk and flesh; man uses the milk to slake his thirst and his flesh to assuage his hunger. And with the energy so provided, he plants more grain and scales mountains. Sunlight, photosynthesis, and respiration sustain all life.

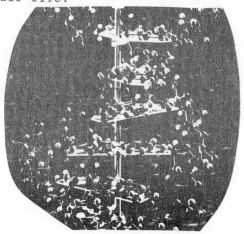

Model of a DNA (deoxyribonucleic acid) molecule.

DRAWING OF A GENERALIZED PLANT CELL

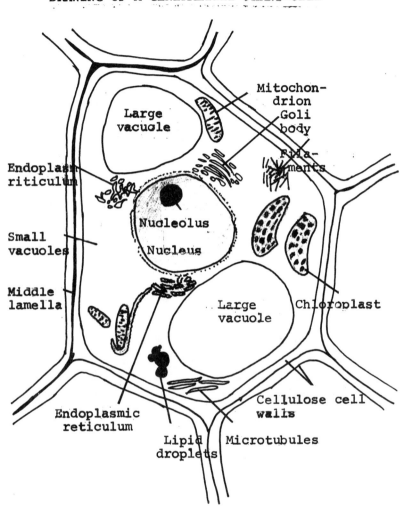

Large
vacuole

Mitochon-
drion

Goli
body

Fila-
ments

Endoplasmic
riticulum

Nucleolus

Nucleus

Small
vacuoles

Middle
lamella

Large
vacuole

Chloroplast

Endoplasmic
reticulum

Cellulose cell
walls

Lipid
droplets

Microtubules

PARENCHYMA CELLS

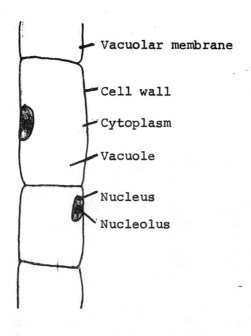

Vacuolar membrane

Cell wall

Cytoplasm

Vacuole

Nucleus

Nucleolus

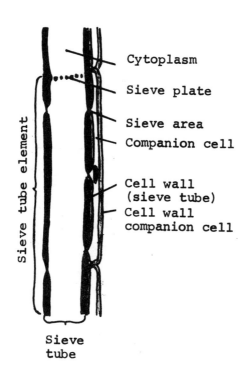

Cytoplasm

Sieve plate

Sieve area
Companion cell

Cell wall
(sieve tube)
Cell wall
companion cell

Sieve tube element

Sieve
tube

ROOT HAIR CELL

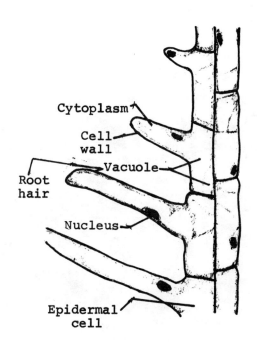

Cytoplasm

Cell
wall

Vacuole

Root
hair

Nucleus

Epidermal
cell

DRAWING OF A GENERALIZED ANIMAL CELL

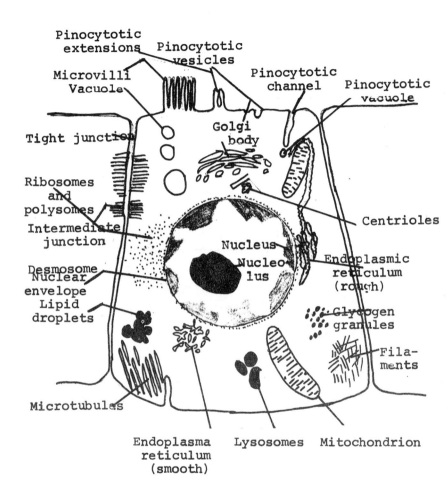

Pinocytotic extensions
Pinocytotic vesicles
Microvilli
Vacuole
Pinocytotic channel
Pinocytotic vacuole
Tight junction
Golgi body
Ribosomes and polysomes
Intermediate junction
Centrioles
Nucleus
Nucleolus
Desmosome
Nuclear envelope
Lipid droplets
Endoplasmic reticulum (rough)
Glycogen granules
Filaments
Microtubules
Endoplasma reticulum (smooth)
Lysosomes
Mitochondrion

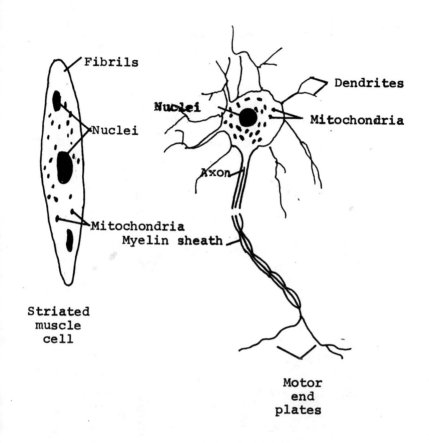

Fibrils

Nuclei

Nuclei

Dendrites

Mitochondria

Axon

Mitochondria
Myelin sheath

Striated
muscle
cell

Motor
end
plates

Motor Neuron

LIVER PARENCHYMAL CELL

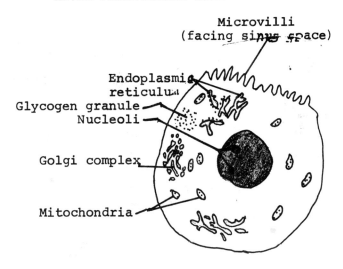

Microvilli
(facing sinus space)

Endoplasmic reticulum

Glycogen granule

Nucleoli

Golgi complex

Mitochondria

KIDNEY CELL (PROXIMAL CONVOLUTED TUBULER)

Microvilli Mitochondria Nucleus Endoplasmic reticulum

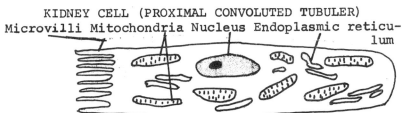

SPERM CELL

Tail filaments   Mitpchondria   Nucleus

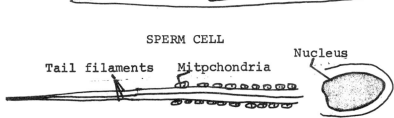

Test your knowledge of competency 4-2.

1. What is the basic unit of all living matter?
   a. plants
   b. animals
   c. cells
   d. tissues

2. The structure of cells are closely related to their
   a. shape
   b. function
   c. size
   d. environment

3. What are the two main regions of plant cells?
   a. cell wall and protoplast
   b. cytoplasm and organelles
   c. vacuoles and molecules
   d. polypacchaude walls and nucleus

4. Cells noted for their mobility and their ability to ingest food particles that are subsequently digested inside the cell are
   a. animal
   b. plant
   c. tissue
   d. nucleus

5. What is the dual miracle of chemistry?
   a. photosynthesis and life
   b. respiration and walking
   c. photosynthesis and respiration
   d. plants and animals

Answers: 1. c, 2. b, 3. a, 4. a, 5. c

Competency 5: Identify the structural organization of organisms in relation to cells, tissues,
and organs.

Cells

The cell is the building block of life. The
typical cell contains a nucleus surrounded by
streaming cytoplasm and is covered by a thin cell
membrane.

The cell membrane controls what enters and
leaves the cell just as the nuclear membrane controls what enters and leaves the nucleus. Things
like food and oxygen enter the cell through the
cell membrane.

Cells multiply by splitting in two. Each
then grows to the size of the original cell by converting food into the kinds of molecules essential
for its structure and functions.

The very simplest animals have bodies composed of a single cell or at best, a loose grouping of more or less similar cells.

These few cells suffice for primitive life
form. However, in those animals which are more
complex in structure, the need for specialization
to meet the demands of the larger body size
becomes increasingly apparent. In human societies
no single individual can be simultaneously a successful plumber, lawyer, artist, a farmer, and
merchant. Likewise, a group of similar cells cannot possibly carry on all the functions of a

complex body. The work of society is conducted by groups of specialists, and the same is true of the work of the human body. Division of labor is accomplished by the specialization of its cells, and of its various tissues and organs.

Tissues

A group of the same kind of cells that do the same kind of work is called a tissue.

The four primary tissues of the human body are epithelium which protects surfaces and absorbs or secretes materials, muscular tissue which is highly contractile, connective tissue which provides support and holds parts together, and nervous tissue which is irritable and conducts impulses. Even blood which is a liquid is a tissue.

Organs

An organ can be defined as a group of tissues which function together in the performance of some vital activity. The tissues in an organ are not necessarily all alike in structure or function, but by the coordination of their individual activities they form a distinct part of the organism.

The hand may be taken as an example of an organ. Here we have a collection of different tissues, all of which work together to give us a very useful part of the body. The outside of the hand is covered by a highly complex type of stratified epithelium which in certain areas have become folded into ridges (the fingertips). These ridges supply a slightly roughened surface to aid in grasping. Embedded in the skin are highly sensitive nerve receptors. Also in the skin and throughout the entire hand are blood vessels that carry the blood to supply the tissues with needed food and oxygen. In the walls of the blood vessels are smooth muscle fibers, while the fingers are moved by the action of striated muscles, many of which are located in the forearm, although there are some in the hand to perform its more delicate motions. Bone and cartilage serve as the supporting elements of the hand, and there is adipose tissue in the palm and elsewhere to absorb shocks. All of these various types of tissues are held together by bands of connective tissue. This is an example of a group of tissues functioning as a coordinated organ.

Systems

A group of organs that work together to carry out a special activity is called a system. The division of labor is accomplished not only by tissues and organs, but on a more elaborate scale by the systems. For example, the digestive system of the human body includes such organs as the esophagus, stomach, liver and intestines.

Test your knowledge of competency 5.

1. A group of cells similar in structure and function is a(n)
   a. organ
   b. system
   c. tissue
   d. organism

2. Although blood is a liquid it is considered to be a
   a. tissue
   b. organ
   c. system
   d. organism

3. The four primary tissues of the human body are
   a. epithelium, muscular, connective, blood
   b. epithelium, muscular, connective, nervous
   c. epithelium, muscular, connective, heart
   d. epithelium, muscular, connective, skin

4. Which of the following is not true?
   a. The cell is the building block of life.
   b. Tissue is a group of the same kind of cells that do the same kind of work.
   c. An organ is a group of tissues which function together in the performance of some vital activity.
   d. A system is a group of organs that work together to carry out a special activity.
   e. None, they are all true statements.

Answers: 1. a, 2. a, 3. b, 4. e

Each tissue cell is uniquely fitted for its job.

33

Competency 6: Describe the function of the parts of an organism and their relation to each other in coordination, reproduction, and growth.

The human body is built on the same plan as a modern skyscraper. There is a rigid internal arrangement of beams and gerders, the skeleton, to which the rest of the structure is attached. The human body has the added feature of flexibility. Its parts can be moved with the help of the muscular system. The long bones are designed as levers that are moved by the muscles attached to the bone framework. Efficient operation of the body requires division of work into different departments, just as in a city or a large industrial plant. These departments of the body are called systems. The skin system serves as the police force protecting the other systems and parts. All the organs concerned with preparing food for the use of the body are part of the digestive system. The circulatory system handles the transportation of materials throughout the body. The respiratory system is made up of the organs that supply oxygen and get rid of certain wastes. The excretory system is the sanitation system of the body, ridding the body of its wastes. The nervous and endocrine systems have as their job that of controlling the body.

A closer look at these systems, their parts and functions will be discussed throughout the remainder of this competency. The systems that will be discussed will be the skin system, skeletal system, muscular system, digestive system, circulatory system, respiratory system, excretory system,

nervous system, endocrine system, and the reproductive system.

The skin system is made up of the skin, hair,
and nails. The skin acts as a protective covering
preventing harmful bacteria from entering the body.
It forms a waterproof covering preventing water
and other liquids from leaving the inner tissues.
The skin also protects the inner parts from
injuries such as bumps, bruises, scratches, and
cuts. The pigment in the skin protects the skin
from the sun's rays. The nerve ending in the skin
makes it sensitive to touch, pressure, pain, heat,
and cold. The sweat glands rid the body of waste
materials and aid the body in controlling and regu-
lating body temperature along with the blood
vessels in the body.

The skeletal system encompasses the various
bones of the body. Their primary function is to
hold the body up and give it shape. It also provides a place for the muscles to be attached,
making it possible to walk, breathe, and eat. The
bones also serve to protect the delicate organs of
the body. For example, the skull protects the
brain, the rib cage protects the heart and lungs,
and the spinal column protects the large nerve
center called the spinal cord.

The muscular system contains more than 400
muscles and their primary job is to cause movement
for the rest of the body. As they move they cause
other parts of the body to move. No movement
occurs or is possible without the use of muscles.

The digestive system is made up of the mouth,
stomach, intestines, and liver. Digestion is
carried on by special organs including the alimen-   •
tary canal, the food tube, and the digestive canal.
The alimentary canal is the passageway through
which the food travels. With the help of the
digestive glands, food is broken up into simpler
dissolved form. Digestion begins in the mouth
which prepares food for digestion. It then travels

to the stomach, which acts as a storage unit for usually 2-3 hours, and prepares the food for digestion in the small intestine. While in the small intestine, food is mixed with juices that contains enzymes to dissolve foods to simpler forms that can be taken in or absorbed through the walls of the small intestine to the blood stream. Food that cannot be used or digested by the body passes through the small intestine to the large intestine as waste materials to be later expelled by the body.

The circulatory system is made up of the heart, blood, and blood vessels. The system has three main functions. The first is to carry digested food to the cells of the body. The second is to bring oxygen to the cells for burning food and providing heat and energy. The third function is to take waste materials produced by the cells to the organs that will expell them. This waste removal is done by either of two systems. One that takes blood to the lungs and returns to the right auricle; or, the second which takes blood to all parts of the body and returns to the left auricle.

The respiratory system includes the nose, windpipe and the lungs. Respiration is described as the action of the cells that produce energy. The function of the respiratory system is to bring oxygen into the body and get rid of carbon dioxide. Inhaled air passes through the nostrils to the nasal passages where the air is moistened, cleaned, and warmed to the body temperature. This keeps the air entering the lungs from damaging them. The air then enters the throat cavity and passes the trapdoor guarding the entrance to the windpipe. The windpipe branches into the bronchi, which by smaller and smaller tubes lead to the lungs. Once the oxygen enters the lungs, the oxygen passes through the walls of the air sacs and capillaries and into the blood. It will eventually be carried to every cell of the body.

The excretory system includes the kidneys and
the bladder. Its functions is to remove waste
materials from the body. This removal can be done
in one of three ways. Through the lungs, carbon
dioxide and water are given off in the form of
water vapor. The skin gives off water and mineral
salts as perspiration. And the kidneys remove
from the blood waste materials such as mineral
salts, and protein compounds. Undigested and
unused food is also expelled through the kidneys.

The human body is under the dual control of
the nervous and endocrine systems. The primary
control is exerted through the nervous system,
whose branching nerves penetrate the entire body
with headquarters housed in the brain. Chemical
control is directed by the endocrine glands,
through the hormones they secrete.

The nervous system is composed of the nerves,
brain, and spinal cord. It serves to control the
muscles and other tissues of the body. It serves
to control the action of the organs. It also controls sensations such as smell, taste, touch,
pressure, sight, hearing, heat, cold, and pain.
Last, the nerves serve to control thinking, learning, and memory.

The endocrine system contains glands that are
organs whose cells give off juices that have special uses to the body. Duct glands give off
juices that travel through the ducts to the parts
they affect. For example, the salivary glands
gives saliva in the mouth. Ductless glands gives
off hormones that travels through the blood to the
different parts of the body. They serve to regu-
late the body activities. These include the
pituitary, thyroid, adrenal, and reproductive
glands.

The reproductive system includes all those
parts affecting sex characteristics and producing
offspring. The male sex organs called testes are
located in the scrotum and produce the sex cells

called sperm. It also produces the hormones that determine the male characteristics which appear during puberty. The female sex organs are called the ovaries and are located in the lower abdomen on each side of the uterus. The ovaries produce sex cells called eggs. It also produces the hormone that attributes for the female characteristics that appear during puberty. The life of a new individual starts with fertilization, the joining of sperm and the egg into a single cell.

Each system of the body has its own distinctive parts and functions. Each is an entity in itself. However, each is also a contributing member to the efficient working machine called the human body.

Test your knowledge of competency 6.

1. The primary function of the skeletal system is to
    a. protect the body
    b. make it possible to breathe
    c. hold the body up and give it shape
    d. control the muscles of the body

2. The human body is under the dual control of which two systems?
    a. the excretory and respiratory systems
    b. the circulatory and skeletal systems
    c. the nervous and endocrine systems
    d. the digestive and skin systems

3. Match the systems in the first column with the functions in the second column.

_____ (1) skin

_____ (2) skeletal

_____ (3) muscular

_____ (4) digestive

_____ (5) circulatory

_____ (6) respiratory

_____ (7) excretory

_____ (8) nervous

_____ (9) endocrine

_____(10) reproductive

a. contains the mouth, stomach, intestines, liver

b. includes the kidneys and the bladder

c. holds the body up, gives the body shape, protects the organs

d. contains testes and ovaries

e. carries food and oxygen to cells, removes waste

f. provides primary control of the body

g. protective covering, prevents bacteria from entering the body

h. provides chemical control of the body through hormones secreted

i. carries oxygen to the body, removes carbon dioxide

j. causes movement

Answers: 1. c, 2. c, 3. (1) g, (2) c, (3) j, (4) a, (5) e, (6) i, (7) b, (8) f, (9) h, (10) d

39

Competency 7: Analyze the interdependence of living things, including identifying the importance of structure, function, growth, and heredity.

Every organism on Earth is a member of an ecosystem, a unit that consists of other organisms that affect it, plus the non-living matter and radiant energy that make up its physical environment. It is easy to think of a pond or an island in the middle of the ocean as a single ecosystem. But it is often equally useful units: a patch of pine forest or the grassy border of a highway. The limits drawn around ecosystems are never entirely closed. All patches of nature are linked to the surrounding environment.

To understand fully this basic principle of ecological energetics, one must understand the nature of the food chain. A food chain is most commonly a sequence of prey and predator species; one species is eaten by another, which is eaten in turn by a third, and so on. Predation is the act of consuming another organism. Predators are either hervivores, carnivores, or omnivores. Predators and prey can control each other's population size. When the prey become too numerous, they are cropped back in a density dependent manner by the predators. When the predators become too numerous, they crop the prey down to a low level, which causes them to run out of food and to suffer a population decline of their own.

Examples of typical food chains from terestrial and marine environments are as follows. A food chain from the grasslands of Canada may

40

consist of a coyote which feeds on a prairie vole which feeds on grass which gets its food from the soil (from bacteria and other decomposers). A marine food chain may consist of a whale which feeds on various types of smaller fish which feed on even smaller fish on down to the zooplankton which would feed on the microscopic phytoplankton.

Each species forms a step, or link as it usually is called, in one or more food chains. The positions located on the food chain are referred to as the trophic level. Thus the green plants, which are the producers for the entire community, comprise the first level. The second level is formed by the herbivores, which are the consumers of the green plants, the third tropic level is formed by the carnivores, which eat the herbivores and the omnivores which eat the herbivores and the producers. The fourth trophic level by the secondary carnivores, which eat the carnivores, and so on. In almost all ecosystems there exist top carnivores--one or more large, specialized animal species that browse on the animals in the lower trophic levels but are not ordinarily consumed by predators themselves. The larger whales enjoy this status, as do lions, wolves and man, the most gluttonous of all the top carnivores. In addition to the producer-to-carnivore chains there are parasite chains which are examples of symbiosis. Biologists define symbiosis as the association of two species in a prolonged and intimate ecological relationship, ordinarily involving frequent or permanent bodily contact. Symbiosis can take one or the other of the following three basic forms: in Parasitism one species benefits at the expense of the other; in Commensalism one species benefits while the other species neither benefits nor is harmed; in Mutualism both species benefit from the relationship. Parasitic symbiosis is involved in the association between the flea and the dog. Symbiosis between tropical fish Aeoliscus strigatus and a sea urchin. The fish is protected by the sheltering spines of the sea urchin without affecting it one way or the other.

Mutualism exists between ants and aphids. When
stroked by the ant's antennac, the aphid excretes
sugar-rich "honey-dew" for the ant. In return,
ants protect aphids from parasitic wasps and other
enemies.

Because of the complexity of the subject, the
study of symbiosis is virtually a science unto
itself. Symbioses of one kind or another occur in
all the major groups of organisms, from protists
to mammals. They are extraordinarily diverse in
kind, and the more advanced types employ bizarre
adaptations that completely transform the life
cycles and even the anatomy of the participants.
As one might expect, the life cycles of symbionts
are the most complex found in nature.

A major goal of education is the recognition
by man of his interdependence with his environment
and with life everywhere, and the development of a
culture that maintains that relationship through
policies and practices necessary to secure the
future of an environment fit for life and fit for
living.

The understanding of interrelationships of
living things with each other and with their
physical environment--the science of ecology--is
the key to sound environment.

A FOOD CHAIN

WHO EATS WHOM?

    Green plants in a field are eaten by mice.
The mice are eaten by hawks. The green plants
are the producers, they manufacture the food.
The mouse is a consumer, it feeds directly on
the plant, so it is a first-order consumer.
The hawk in this food chain is a second-order
consumer.

43

A FOOD WEB

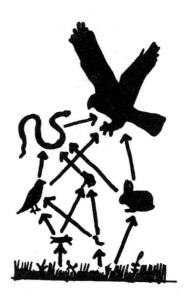

A simple food web suggest the complex
interrelationships of living things. The simple
food chain branches to become a food web,
which is closer to the true pattern of nature.
Food chains and webs constitute a natural system
of checks and balances. If for some reason
one type of animal multiplies rapidly, their
numbers will be diminished by predation of
others.

44

A SIMPLE FOOD WEB

A PYRAMID OF NUMBERS

Each level depends on the broader one under it for a supply of food.

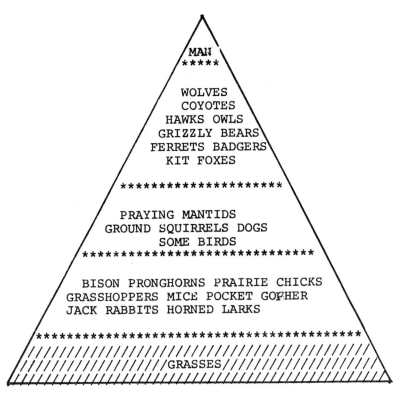

Ecologists have constructed pyramids for large regions called biomes, which are communities of living things associated with a particular kind of vegetation typical of the area. A grassland or prairie pyramid is above. Other biomes are the tundra of the artic, the tropical rainforest, and various grasslands.

Test your knowledge of competency 7.

1. Omnivores are on the third trophic level and eat
    a. producers
    b. herbivores
    c. carnivores
    d. both a and b
    e. both b and c

2. Commensalism is a form of symbiosis that exists when
    a. one species benefits and the other is harmed
    b. one species benefits and the other is neither harmed nor helped
    c. both species benefit from the relationship
    d. neither species benefit

3. Predators are either
    a. hervivores
    b. carnivores
    c. omnivores
    d. a, b, and c

4. An ecosystem contains
    a. b, c, and d
    b. organisms
    c. non-living matter
    d. radiant energy

5. The association of two species in a prolonged and intimate ecological relationship is
    a. mutualism
    b. symbiosis
    c. mitosis
    d. parasitism

Answers: 1. d, 2. b, 3. d, 4. a, 5. b

Competency 8: Identify human health problems related to communicable diseases, drugs, alcohol, and tobacco.

Communicable Disease

Communicable disease is a sickness that is passed along from a sick person to a healthy one. This may be done directly, through some third person, or through an animal or object. These diseases may be caused by different organisms including viruses, bacteria, fungi, and protozoa. Communicable diseases are spread by the air, people both directly and indirectly, animals, insects, water, food, and soil.

Three communicable diseases which are common health problems in the United States are mononucleosis, hepatitis, and venereal diseases. Mononucleosis is believed to be caused by a virus and spread from person to person by direct or indirect contact. Symptoms of mononucleosis are like those to many mild illnesses, thus causing a person to wait weeks before going to the doctor. Organs such as the liver and the spleen may be affected causing other parts of the body not to function as they should. A person usually tires very easily with mononucleosis. It is curable with medication and plenty of rest.

Hepatitis is a swelling or soreness of the liver caused by what is thought to be a virus. One kind of hepatitis, known as infectious hepatitis, may be spread by unclean food or water. Its symptoms include loss of appetite, upset

48

stomach, headache, fever, and the yellowing of the whites of the eyes and of the skin known as jaundice. Infectious hepatitis may last from one to six weeks. Serum hepatitis has similar symptoms as the infectious type, but they tend to develop more slowly and last longer. A person may have serum hepatitis for many years without showing any symptoms, and therefore spread the disease to others.

Venereal diseases have become one of the biggest health problems in the United States. Syphilis and gonorrhea, the two most common types, are the result of bacterial infections which are transmitted almost entirely by direct contact with an infected person. Both diseases are treated with penicillin during their early stages and may be cured. Gonorrhea may cause damage to the female reproductive system leading to sterility. Its symptoms include a burning feeling when urine is eliminated from the body and the presence of a whitish substance from the vagina of the female or the penis of the male. The first symptom of syphilis, the more serious of the two diseases, is a chancre, or painless sore, which develops on the sex organ at the point where the bacteria entered the body. Other mild symptoms may include fever, sore throat, headache, or rash. The period of communicability for syphilis may last up to one year, after which the disease usually becomes inactive. Many years later the effects of untreated syphilis may include arthritis, blindness, paralysis, insanity, and death.

Communicable diseases are not the serious health problems to the people of the United States that they once were. Diptheria, smallpox, typhoid fever, and tuberculosis have been among the leading causes of death in the past. Today communicable diseases are under greater control due to increased knowledge in the medical field. Health practices which are advised in most educational programs to fight communicable diseases include proper nutrition, adequate rest, regular medical

49

checkups, and immunization against diseases such as polio, flu, and smallpox.

Drugs

Drug abuse, or the taking of drugs for reasons other than health, can result in health problems, both psychological and physical.

Psychological Health Problems

Continued abuse of a drug may cause an emotional need for the drug, known as psychological dependence. Psychological dependence may occur with a wide range of drugs including narcotics, barbiturates, amphetamines, LSD, and marijuana. People who continually abuse drugs often have some sort of mental illness or emotional problem. For those with serious disorders, continual drug abuse may lead to psychosis. A psychotic is one with a permanent disorder of the mind who has lost complete contact with reality.

Physical Health Problems

Physical dependence exists when a person takes a drug several times, developing a need for it which is more important to that person than eating or sleeping. Physical dependence may be caused by narcotics and barbiturates. Amphetamines, LSD, and marijuana do not cause a person to be physically dependent.

Tolerance occurs as a person's body gets used to a drug through repeated doses. Over a period of time larger doses are required to produce the same effect. Large doses increase the chance of damaging a person's mind and/or body. When a person who has a physical dependence on a drug stops taking the drug, the person suffers from withdrawal illness. Withdrawal illness from narcotics may result in watery eyes, abdominal cramps, leg cramps, muscle aches, hot and cold flashes, and excessive yawning. Vomiting, diarrhea, and fever may also occur. Withdrawal illness from barbiturates causes headaches, nervousness, nausea, delirium, and convulsions.

An overdose, or taking too much of a drug, may cause poisoning. Some people recover from drug poisoning, but very often it results in death.

The abuse of drugs may cause disease. When drugs are injected, bacterial and viral infections may be caused by the use of hypodermic syringes that have not been sterilized. Since 1967 there has been a great increase in the number of cases of hepatitis in the United States caused by two or more people using the same syringe.

Respiratory infections and diseases are common among drug abusers. Many narcotic addicts are easily infected and often die from pneumonia. Bronchitis may be caused by smoking hashish over a period of time. Respiratory diseases also occur when even the weaker forms of marijuana are smoked for a great length of time.

Alcohol

Alcohol, probably the oldest drug known, has been used at least since the earliest societies for which records exist. People drink alcohol in three main kinds of beverages: beers, wines, and distilled beverages. Drinkers may become addicted to any of these beverages.

The effects of alcohol on the human body depend on the amount of alcohol in the blood. This varies with rate of consumption and with the rate at which the drinker's physical system absorbs and metabolizes alcohol. After alcohol passes through the stomach, it is rapidly absorbed through the walls of the intestines into the bloodstream and carried to the various organ systems of the body, where it is metabolized.

Alcohol begins to impair the brain's ability to function when the blood-alcohol concentration (BAC) reaches 0.05%. Most state traffic laws in the United States presume that a driver with a BAC of 0.10% is intoxicated. With a concentration of 0.20%, a person has difficulty controlling the emotions and may cry or laugh extensively. The person will experience a great deal of difficulty in attempting to walk and will want to lie down. When the BAC reaches about 0.30% the drinker will have trouble comprehending and may become unconscious. Concentrations above 0.50% may cause death, although a person generally becomes unconscious before absorbing a lethal dosage.

The effects of excessive drinking on major organ systems of the human body are cummulative and become evident after heavy, continuous drinking or after intermittent drinking over a period of time that may range from 5 to 30 years. The parts of the body most affected by heavy drinking are the digestive and nervous systems. Digestive-system disorders that may be related to heavy drinking include cancer of the mouth, throat, and esophagus; gastritis; ulcers; cirrhosis of the liver; and inflammation of the pancreas. Disorders of the nervous system can include neuritis, lapse of memory (blackouts), hallucinations, and extreme tremor as found in delirium tremens. Delirium tremens ("the DTs") may occur when a person stops drinking after a period of heavy, continuous consumption. Permanent damage to the brain and central nervous system may also result. Recent evidence indicates that pregnant women who drink heavily may give birth to infants with the fetal alcohol syndrome, which is characterized by face and body abnormalities and, in some cases, impaired intellectual facilities.

The damaging effects of alcohol are much greater if the drinker is also using drugs. The combination of alcohol and sleeping pills has sometimes been fatal, even when both are taken in non-lethal doses. Other commonly used drugs such as tranquilizers, antibiotics, aspirin, and even old remedies have been found to interact dangerously with alcohol.

Drinking behavior differs significantly among groups of different age, sex, social class, racial status, ethnic background, occupational status, religious affiliation, and regional location. The way people drink varies with their status in society.

Moderate or temperate use of alcohol is not harmful, but excessive or heavy drinking is associated with alcoholism. The alcoholic is a very sick person whose life is in danger.

Alcohol-related pamphlets, books, posters and other materials published by the National Institute on Alcohol Abuse and Alcoholism can be obtained free of charge in limited quantities. The address is: NCALI, P.O. Box 2345, Rockville, Maryland 20852.

Tobacco

Medical studies show that smoking is a great health hazard because of its effects on the body. These studies show that the average life expectancy of a smoker is three to four years less than that of a nonsmoker. The life expectancy of a heavy smoker--a person who smokes two or more packages of cigarettes a day--may be as much as eight years shorter than that of a nonsmoker.

Smoking has significant effects on the body because of (1) the nicotine in tobacco, (2) the tars in tobacco, and (3) smoke particles that are trapped in the lungs.

The beginning smoker often has symptoms of mild nicotine poisoning--dizziness, faintness, rapid pulse, cold, clammy skin, and sometimes nausea, vomiting, and diarrhea. For most people, smoking reduces the appetite and dulls the sense of taste and smell. A cigar, cigarette, or a pipe after meals may cause chronic digestive disturbances.

The most notable effect of nicotine is a transient stimulation followed by depression of both the sympathetic and the central nervous systems. This feeling of stimulation is followed by depression and further fatigue.

Tobacco smoke contains substances which irritate the mucus membrane of the respiratory tract and it is well known that excessive smoking causes cough, hoarseness, bronchitis, and other related conditions. Studies show that respiratory illnesses are nine times as frequent for smokers than nonsmokers. Nose and throat specialists can easily identify a smoker by the irritated inflamant appearance of the mucous membranes of the nose and pharynx.

The heart rate increases after smoking. Blood pressure usually rises and the small arteries contract and reduces the flow of blood.

Studies have shown that cigarette smoking or the injection of nicotine stimulates the adrenal gland to produce increased amounts of hormones. which affect the action of other organs and other glands of internal secretion.

Cancer of the lung is the leading cause of cancer deaths. Other cancers caused by smoking are cancer of the lip, tongue, pharynx, larynx, esophagus, pancreas, liver, urinary bladder, stomach, and kidneys.

Buerger's disease, a rare but serious disease of the blood vessels, has long been recognized as due primarily to the use of tobacco. In this disease, blood flow to the extremities is progressively reduced. In advanced cases, gangrene frequently occurs and amputation of the affected part becomes necessary.

The most frequent cause of death in the country is coronary heart disease. There is a definite association between this disease and cigarette smoking. Coronary heart disease occurs when a coronary artery or one of its branches becomes plugged or obstructed.

Many smokers develop emphysema, a disease that destroys the walls of the air sacs of the lungs. Emphysema reduces the surface area of the lungs through which oxygen and carbon dioxide can pass, causing serious shortness of breath.

Early medical evidence supports the health hazard of smoking. Dr. Evard of London, 300 years ago, said smoking causes one to loose his temper beyond bounds of health, it causes vomiting, and is an enemy of the stomach. A century ago Bouisson did a clinical study of 68 cases of cancer of the oral cavities in a hospital in France. All the patients used tobacco in one form or other.

Test your knowledge of competency 8.

1. Which of the following communicable diseases is not a major problem to the people of the United States?
    a. hepatitis
    b. syphilis
    c. malaria
    d. mononucleosis

2. Of all communicable diseases, syphilis is known to be one of the most serious because
    a. it spreads more readily than any other disease by way of direct personal contact, air, and insects
    b. it cannot be treated except in rare cases
    c. when left untreated it may cause blindness, paralysis, insanity, and even death
    d. all of the above

3. Which of the following is not a health problem related to drugs?
   a. physical dependence
   b. poisoning
   c. hepatitis
   d. aging

4. Physical dependence on drugs may be caused when which of the following are abused?
   a. narcotics
   b. marijuana
   c. barbiturates
   d. both a and c

5. A person is considered intoxicated if the blood-alcohol concentration is
   a. 0.05%
   b. 0.10%
   c. 0.20%
   d. 0.30%

6. The parts of the body most affected by heavy drinking are the
   a. circulatory system
   b. skeletal system
   c. digestive and nervous system
   d. lungs

7. A person who stops drinking after a period of heavy, continuous consumption may develop
   a. neuritis
   b. ulcers
   c. lapse of memory
   d. DTs

8. The poisonous substance in tobacco is
   a. opium
   b. marijuana
   c. nicotine
   d. lead poison

9.   Smoking reduces the appetite and dulls the
     senses of
     a.   touch and taste
     b.   sight and smell
     c.   taste and smell
     d.   smell and sight

10.   Buerger's disease is a serious disease of the
      a.   heart
      b.   blood vessels
      c.   lungs
      d.   intestines

Answers: 1.   c, 2.   c, 3.   d, 4.   d, 5.   b,
           6.   c, 7.   d, 8.   c, 9.   c, 10.   b

Competency 9: Demonstrate appropriate knowledge of safety principles related to school, home, and community.

School

I. School safety principles are designed to guide school administrators, teachers, and other members of the staff in recognizing environmental hazards, in taking steps to control and eliminate them, in utilizing both curricular and cocurricular activities, and in enlisting the cooperation of all school personnel in all phases of school safety.

II. School safety programs should create and make effective use of school safety organizations, particularly student patrols.

   A. Student safety organizations help prevent school accidents and help develop social and civic responsibility.

      1. A school may set up a junior safety council to function as a clearing-house for all safety matters brought to its attention, to coordinate the various school activities concerned with accident prevention, and to establish safety regulations governing such matters as the use of bicycles and motor vehicles and the conduct of students in halls, stairways, and play areas.

2. School safety patrols have saved many school children from injury and death through offering protection for youngsters on their way to and from school, in the school building, on the school bus, and on the playground.

3. The building patrol helps maintain safe and orderly movement of the student body within the school building and provides information and guidance for pupils and visitors.

4. The bus patrol assists in keeping order among pupil riders, and in aiding students to board and leave buses and to cross the highway safely at bus stops under supervision of the bus driver.

5. A civil defense patrol provides an additional stabilizing force during civil defense or security drills, helps in the exchange of vital information between the principal's office and the classrooms, and is prepared to assist in an emergency.

6. An exit-drill patrol or fire-drill patrol assists in the safe and orderly clearing of pupils from the building.

7. The playground patrol helps to keep play areas in good condition, checks to see that students use play equipment correctly, and keeps children within the proper play areas.

8. The traffic patrol instructs and protects members of the student body in crossing the streets and highways at or near schools.

III. Adult crossing guards are employed in a large number of school districts to protect school children who must cross hazardous intersections on their way to and from school.

IV. Since thousands of youngsters travel to and from school on bicycles, it is a responsibility of the schools to develop a bicycle safety program that will provide for safety on the school grounds and educational experience in the proper care and operation of bicycles.

    A. Bicycle safety on the school grounds is relatively simple to achieve.

        1. There should be a specific and rigidly enforced rule that forbids bicycle riding on the school grounds.

        2. Adequate storage racks should be made available so that the students will have a place to park their bicycles safely and conveniently.

        3. Bicycle inspection tests will determine the condition of the vehicle, the riding skills of the students, and the knowledge of the student concerning rules of the road and safe riding practices.

    B. Due to the instruction given in good bicycle safety programs at schools, there has been a considerable reduction in the number of fatalities and injuries during recent years.

V. Since so many students travel to school in buses and private cars, it is necessary for the school to make provisions for safe loading and unloading of passengers.

A. Eliminate as many traffic hazards as pos-
    sible by passing and enforcing adequate
    legislation and by improving highways.

    1. School plants should provide ade-
        quate off-street parking and
        passenger loading facilities for
        both buses and cars.

    2. School buses should have regular
        stalls for loading and unloading
        students with supervision provided.

    3. An educational program for parents
        should be implemented to encourage
        use of safe practices when picking
        up pupils.

    4. Students should be instructed in
        methods of passenger loading and
        unloading to prevent running between
        cars or jaywalking across busy
        streets.

B. Every school bus driver should be trained
    for operating a school bus and in
    improved safety procedures.

C. Students should be taught to behave cor-
    rectly when entering, leaving, and
    riding on the bus.

D. The school should organize an effective
    school-bus patrol to assist children in
    entering and leaving the bus, to super-
    vise them during the trip to and from
    school, and to direct the driver when he
    has to maneuver the bus in close quarters
    or at dangerous intersections.

E. Safe, modern buses should be used and
    checked daily by the driver and inspected
    completely at regular intervals, at
    least three times a year, by a competent

mechanic.

F. Drills should be conducted to ensure emergency evacuation of the bus in the event of an accident, fire or the driver's inability to function.

VI. A safe school environment is an important part of a total school safety program.

A. Accidents in and around school account for a large percentage of all the accidents to young people.

1. It has been established that the school is responsible for the child from the time he leaves for school until he returns home.

2. Ensuring safe conditions throughout the school building and grounds is a responsibility of all administrators, teachers, and custodians.

3. Many of the precautions in dealing with safety in the home, vocational safety, and fire prevention can also be applied at school.

B. Selection of the school site is an integral part of school plant planning.

1. In the location of new schools, primary consideration must be given to present and future school populations to determine the potential use of school facilities.

2. Sites should be selected so that students will be confronted with the least possible traffic congestion going to and from school.

3. Other safety factors to be considered

are available means of fire protection and the adequacy and convenience of public transportation facilities.

4. New buildings must meet the highest specifications for safety; safety should not be sacrificed in the interest of economy.

   a. All precautions should be used to provide for fire protection.

   b. Fire-resistant materials should be used.

   c. Fire walls and fire doors should be included where necessary.

   d. Appropriate exits should be provided.

   e. Fire warning and fire-fighting devices should be installed.

   f. Heating and storage rooms should be properly located and protected.

   g. Large assembly rooms should be located on the ground floor.

   h. Adequate ventilating systems should be provided.

   i. Lighting should meet recommended standards.

   j. Appropriate furniture and equipment should be selected for all school buildings.

   k. Existing school buildings should be checked for faulty heating systems, defective wiring, inadequate exits, unsafe floor and stair surfaces, and adequate fire-warning devices and fire-fighting equipment.

C. Approximately one fifth of all school accidents occur on the school grounds.

   1. The school grounds require constant attention if they are to be kept clear of hazards.

   2. School personnel should supervise play areas, furnish adequate instruction in all activities, and inspect the playground thoroughly every day to see that it is free of holes, sharp objects, and rubbish and that all equipment is in good operating condition.

   3. The area should be as level as possible, well drained, and large enough to accommodate all students who are likely to use it at one time.

   4. If it is located near a busy street, it should be enclosed by a fence.

   5. Permanent play equipment should be set up around the sides of the area rather than in the center so that operation of the equipment will not interfere with one another.

   6. Student playground patrols can assist teachers in supervising students during recess and lunch periods to stop dangerous behavior, report damaged or broken equipment, and help custodians keep the grounds clear of debris.

D. Students should be safety-conscious, concerned not only about their own welfare but about that of others.

   1. Well-defined rules of behavior should be set up for use in the school building as well as on the playground.

   2. Accidents at school often occur in the shop, the science laboratory, and the gymnasium.

   3. Students should be alert to hazards in these places and aware of safety practices that may prevent accidents there.

      a. Safety in the shop

         (1) Be sure you are doing your work in an area that allows sufficient space for it.

         (2) If sharing work space with another person, be sure that he will not be hurt by tools, equipment, or material that you are using.

         (3) Before beginning any work, be sure you have planned your work steps and assembled the work materials and equipment needed.

         (4) Use the correct tools for the job at hand.

         (5) Be wary of dull tools.

         (6) Keep tools in safe places when not using them for the moment.

(7) Always read instructions carefully before using any tool or equipment.

(8) Get help from the instructor before using any tool that puzzles you.

b. Safety in the laboratory

(1) Always follow directions in mixing chemicals or in doing experiments.

(2) Handle test tubes and beakers carefully to prevent breakage and spilling of contents, especially when heated.

(3) Report any cracked or chipped apparatus.

(4) Never use beakers for drinking glasses since there may be a chemical residue in them.

(5) Spilled chemicals should be swept up or flushed away immediately.

(6) Hands should be washed at the end of each period.

(7) Always test the gas cock to see that the gas in turned off at the end of the lab period.

(8) Avoid forcing glass tubing into rubber stoppers.

(9) In case a chemical splashes on the skin, wash the skin

immediately with clear water
for at least five minutes.

(10) Should a chemical be
splashed in the eye, the eye
should be washed in running
water for a minimum of ten
minutes and then seen by an
opthalmologist immediately.

(11) Never perform any experiments
in the laboratory when the
instructor is not present.

(12) Avoid sniffing chemicals.

(13) For each experiment, follow
directions about disposing
of wastes since they are possible causes of fires and
explosions.

(14) An apron should be worn to
protect clothing when doing
chemical experiments.

(15) A face and eye shield must
always be worn and rubber
gloves used when handling
irritating chemicals.

c. Safety in the gymnasium

(1) To avoid danger of tripping,
be sure that gym shoes are
fastened securely.

(2) To avoid bruises, cuts, or
scratches, remove rings,
bracelets, and watches before
taking part in physical
education classes.

(3) Before starting a game, note

and correct any possible safety hazards.

(4) In the locker room, do not run, stand on benches, or snap towels.

(5) Keep locker doors closed when they are not in use.

(6) Practice good sportsmanship during games, for upset emotions and poor attitudes may make you more susceptible to accidents.

c. Safety in the school plant

(1) Walk safely through halls, on stairways, and around chairs, desks, and other objects.

(2) Carry chairs, working materials, and other equipment safely in the classroom, in halls, and on stairs.

(3) Avoid pushing, crowding, and running in the building.

(4) Refrain from interfering with anyone who is using the drinking fountain.

(5) Avoid using the toilet rooms as play areas.

(6) Observe clean and orderly habits.

(7) Observe safety procedures, rules, and regulations in play areas and in going to

and from play areas.

    (8) Play only in areas desig-
nated for their own age
group.

    (9) Help keep play areas clean
and safe by removing glass,
sticks, stones, and rubbish.

    (10) Develop a safety sportsman-
ship code applicable to play
areas.

    (11) Participate in organizing
playground and school-
building patrols and obey
such patrols.

    (12) Observe the proper procedure
if an accident should occur.

    (13) Recognize hazards in and
around the school.

E. Every school building should have a well-
developed plan for evacuation in time of
fire or other disaster.

    1. A plan for fire drills should be
developed and numerous practice
drills should be conducted during
the year.

    2. The school administrator should work
closely with the fire department in
setting up a fire-drill program.

    3. All school students and employees
should be told what to do in case of
a fire alarm.

    4. Everyone should participate in fire
drills regardless of what he is doing.

5. Fire drills should not be announced in advance.

6. Fire drills should be conducted during assemblies, while classes are passing, and at lunch periods, as well as during regular class periods.

7. No one should re-enter the building until an appropriate signal is given.

8. Fire drills should be held under circumstances where an exit is blocked and the students must be rerouted to another exit.

F. The use of accident reporting systems established as part of a well-rounded safety program can help the school administrator reduce the number of accidents through effective planning and improvements in the environment.

Test your knowledge of competency 9: safety at school.

1. Accidents occurring on the school grounds make up what percentage of all school accidents?
   a. 10%
   b. 20%
   c. 30%
   d. 50%

2. There has been a considerable reduction in the number of fatalities and injuries due to bicycle accidents chiefly because of
   a. elimination of bicycles from school grounds
   b. age limits on students riding bicycles
   c. instruction in good bicycle safety programs at schools
   d. traffic patrols located at streets or highways at or near schools

3.   Additional help extended to school administrators and teachers during emergency drills may come from
a.   civil defense patrols
b.   firemen
c.   policemen
d.   custodians

Answers: 1. b, 2. c, 3. a

Home

Statistics have shown that in the home, more than in any other area of the community, numerous accidents occur every day. Approximately 27,500 persons are killed in home accidents each year, an average of 74 people per day. The National Safety Council reports that 4.1 million people are injured in the home each year. Also, one out of every forty home injuries results in some form of permanent disability. The principal victims are under 5 years of age and over 65.

The major types of injuries in the home are falls, fire burns, suffocation, poisoning, firearms, and poison gases.

Falls represent the most serious threat in the home. Each year nearly 12,200 persons die because of falls that could have been prevented.

Fire is the second-most frequent accident in the home and is a very serious threat to home life. Each year approximately 6,100 persons are killed in home fires.

During an average year nearly 3,200 persons die from suffocation. Approximately 1,500 deaths occur each year to children under four years of age due to this terrible home accident.

Accidental poisoning occurs in an estimated 250,000 persons each year. Of this number about

1,400 die. Here again, children under four are the most frequent victims.

Firearm accidents in or on home premises cause approximately 1,200 deaths annually. Most of these deaths are caused by carelessness.

Deaths due to gas poisoning take place at an average rate of 2 per day. In a typical year some 800 Americans lose their lives from this cause.

There are other important types of home accidents that are definite threats to the family. There are 2,600 home deaths occurring annually due to drowning, electrocution, burns from hot substances, and blows from falling objects.

Since it appears that home accidents like all other accidents are generally the result of inadequate knowledge, the objectives of the home safety program should be:

1. To train students to recognize the many hazards in the home.

2. To help them develop responsibility toward safeguarding themselves and others against the possibility of home accidents.

3. To train them to perform household tasks safely.

4. To help them acquire safe, orderly habits in the home.

Instruction in home safety can be integrated with other school subjects. For example, a unit dealing with household poisons can be included in a chemistry course; the correct use of knives and other kitchen utensils can be taught in a home economics class; and the safe use of electricity can be covered in a shop course.

Each of the different home accidents should
be discussed and after the students have been
taught to recognize the causes of falls, burns,
and other common accidents, they should be
assigned activities that will aid them in acquir-
ing the attitudes and skills necessary to eliminate these causes.

Some activities that can help students learn
the proper methods of coping with home hazards are:

1. List the various areas in your home--
   stairways, living room, kitchen, bedrooms,
   bathroom, basement, closets, attics,
   porches, yard, garage--and note the
   hazards you discover in each area.

2. List the unsafe practices of various
   members of your family, including your-
   self. Discuss the best ways of overcom-
   ing these practices.

3. Arrange for local radio and television
   publicity as part of a community drive
   to prevent home accidents.

Although most people are aware of some of the
potential dangers in their homes, few take effective remedial action. And the national statistics
on home accidents show no downward trend from year
to year. Perhaps as all phases of accident prevention are increasingly emphasized, people will
develop a generally better attitude toward safety
in all areas of living, including the home.

Some of the important safety practices that
should be taught to students are as follows.

In the kitchen:

1. Maintain clean dry floors at all times.

2. Keep handles of cooking utensils turned
   inward on the stove.

3. Keep electrical appliances away from sinks containing water.

In the bathroom:

1. Use non-skid mats in showers, tubs, and on the floors.

2. Mark poisons and keep out of children's reach.

3. Have a good first-aid kit available.

In stairways and halls:

1. Light all stairways and halls adequately.

2. Provide railings and banisters and keep in good repair.

3. Use gates at head and foot of stairways to protect small children.

In the bedroom:

1. Never smoke in bed.

2. Turn off gas heaters before going to bed.

3. Install lamps or light switches near beds to be reached safely in the dark.

In the living room:

1. Provide snug-fitting metal screens for fireplaces.

2. Anchor all rugs with non-skid materials.

3. Inspect all flues, pipes, and chimneys regularly.

In the attic, basement and garage:

1. Dispose of all rubbish and inflammable litter on a regular schedule.

2. Keep each place well-lighted.

3. Open garage doors when running vehicle motor inside.

Test your knowledge of competency 9: safety at home.

1. The most frequent accident in the home is
    a. poisoning
    b. falls
    c. electrocution
    d. fire burns

2. The second most frequent accident in the home is due to
    a. suffocation
    b. firearms
    c. fire
    d. electrocution

3. The majority of home accidents are a result of
    a. inadequate knowledge
    b. burns
    c. drowning
    d. carelessness

4. Most accidents in the home happen to this age group
    a. 25-40 years of age
    b. birth to one year
    c. under 4 years and over 65 years of age
    d. over 65

5. National statistics show
    a. a downward trend in home accidents
    b. no downward trend in home accidents
    c. about the same numbers year after year
    d. an increase in home accidents

Answers: 1. b, 2. c, 3. a, 4. c, 5. b

Community

A community is defined as: a number of people having common ties or interests, living in the same place and subject to the same laws. These laws also protect the people from disasters, both natural and man-made.

A disaster is technically defined as any sudden, unforeseen emergency such as tornado, flood, fire, riot, hurricane, earthquake, or explosion that will or may cause personal injury, loss of life and/or property damage, including an act of war.

The most devastating disaster on record in the United States is the Galveston tidal wave on September 8, 1900, in which 6,000 people lost their lives.

How can we prepare our community for disasters that may affect us in the future?

First, every individual must prepare himself in his own mind. This includes whether or not a person knows what to do in a community disaster, the wisdom they use, their emotional security, and whether or not they can defend themselves.

There are several types of disasters:

1. Military attack. This includes not only war, but also the atom bomb attack. The Civil Defense of America has always been a large promoter of community preparedness. To aid in military attacks they have sponsored meetings in which they give helpful instruction as to the steps to take in an attack.

Most all communities provide fallout shelters for their citizens in the event of a nuclear war. These shelters are kept stocked with food, water, and other necessities that would be needed by its residences.

2. Natural Disasters. Natural disasters are generally of two types:

    (1) Those caused by nature.

    (2) Those caused by negligent or willful acts of man.

Mother nature can be very cruel. When a natural disaster strikes, the loss of property and lives can be great. Those disasters that are referred to as natural are: (1) hurricane, (2) tornado, (3) flood, (4) earthquake, and (5) blizzard.

Community protection from each of these disasters is available. The American Red Cross has always been a primary helper where these are concerned. The Red Cross offers first aid classes and other services to communities.

Blood drives sponsored by the Red Cross are held year round to insure citizens of the community that blood will be available should they need it.

Colleges can also play an important role in insuring the protection of its community. First aid classes are included in the curriculum of many colleges as well as fire prevention and traffic control.

Those disasters that are termed man made are: (1) fire, (2) automobile accidents, (3) explosions, and (4) riots.

Fortunately, most communities are safeguarded when any one of those disasters strikes. Fire departments are more qualified and trained than ever before to tackle even the most outrageous fire. Each year, thousands of dollars are spent, even in the smallest of communities, on fire fighting equipment.

Trained paramedics are now available today to

aid victims in auto accidents. No longer does the injured victim have to wait until they reach the hospital to receive help.

Police are also highly qualified to deal with riots more than ever before. In their training, they are taught how to deal with riotous people and how to aid those who are injured as a result.

Although no one has found the answer as to how to end disasters, and surely never will, we as citizens of our individual communities can rest in the fact that there are those to help us in our time of need.

Test your knowledge of competency 9: safety in the community.

1. Which of the following is (are) considered natural disasters?
    A. those caused by nature
    b. those caused by negligent or willful acts of man
    c. both a and b
    d. neither a nor b

2. Which of the following is (are) considered man made disasters?
    a. fire
    b. flood
    c. blizzard
    d. earthquake

3. Which of the following best describes what a fallout shelter provides for its residences?
    a. water
    b. food
    c. books to read
    d. most necessities

Answers: 1. c, 2. a, 3. d

Competency 10: Describe human influences on natural systems. For example: identify artificial changes in atmosphere, soil, and water; analyze the consequences of change in relation to the natural system.

Manipulation of the environment to benefit human beings is at least as old as Judeo-Christian teachings and probably as old as human societies. In economic terms, the environment has been regarded as a free good; for most of our history we have used as much of it to absorb wastes as was necessary or desired.

In the broadest sense, water can be described as "polluted" when it is enriched with any kind of nutrient. This definition does not include many types of natural enrichment such as estuaries trapping nutrients carried downstream. To most people the term "water pollution" raises images of sewage flowing into a river, chemical wastes pouring into a lake, or closed beaches and massive fish kills; in short, water pollution is blamed on sophisticated industrial chemicals and vast volumes of sewage. At least we must conclude that the scale and effects of human-related water pollution are overwhelming compared with all natural sources.

Consider any body of water. When members of the aquatic community die they are decomposed by bacteria, fungi, and aquatic insects. Some of these compounds will enrich plant growth and some will be washed away. These cycles of decomposition are sensitive to disturbance. If there is a large pulse of organic matter introduced into the system, decomposer activity may increase so dramatically that they use all available oxygen in the water; other organisms suffocate, and the whole system breaks down. Human organic wastes can be expected to have the same effect. Substances like mercury and DDT--which are active biologically--are readily incorporated into food chains and are dangerous poisons. Other substances, like insoluble inorganic salts, may be so chemically and biologically inert that they constitute no substantial danger.

Pollution usually induces physical and chemical changes in the water. The use of non-biodegradable detergents in the 1950's is an example. It caused a foam in streams. The addition of pollutants in water can cut light penetration and in turn affect photosynthesis.

Changes in heat balance are far more dangerous. If a nuclear power plant is located on a lake, it's waste heat can modify the internal circulation patterns and temperature stratification to the detriment of the lake.

The role of natural ecosystems in the destruction of air pollutants is much smaller than we have seen for water, if only because the air is sparsely inhabited. The internal combustion engine is most recognized by the public as the modern villain that has supplanted the smokestack and the steel mill.

As a result of chemicals being released into the atmosphere we're seeing more instances of "acid rain" throughout Europe and North America. These hydrated pollutants in turn destroy plant and animal life as well as causing corrosion and erosion. Our society is so dependent upon the very industrialization that produces these pollutants that the problem can and will not be easily corrected.

The physical properties of some pollutants can have enormous effect on weather and climate. Certain areas receive excessive rainfall due to the heavy output of particular materials from smokestacks. The particles act as condensation nuclei. The result can also produce extensive cloud formation and reduce sunlight penetration to the extent of damaging crops and plants.

Human health is another area greatly influenced by air pollutants. It seems probable that air pollution acts in a manner like cigarette smoking. One might expect a higher incidence of lung and heart diseases.

Fortunately, chemical contamination of the atmosphere is a steady-state phenomenon that would decline naturally if rates of pollution generation were decreased.

To increase the total supply of food, more land must be put into production, or productivity per acre must be raised. With the first alternative, less land will be available to support natural systems; they are replaced by simplified systems that are inherently unstable. On the other hand, increasing yields per acre bears a different kind of environmental cost; the need to use more pesticides and higher rates of fertilizer application, and, as a result, runoff of water loaded with salts and pesticides that can then pollute other environments. However, because environmental costs either can be ignored or passed on to someone else, it is not surprising that these kinds of major costs have not been included in economic analyses of decision-making regarding agriculture and population growth. As long as a city is growing, supply and demand for land to build upon generates rising values that promote conversion of agricultural land to urban uses; farmers then can take part of their profits and move their operations to cheaper land farther from the city. Higher transportation costs can be passed on to consumers, while other costs would be expected to be the same. The real loser is the environment, if only because another piece of marshland, prairie-chicken habitat, or native wild grasses is irretrievably lost, or because large quantities of potent pesticides are used to the detriment of organisms in surrounding habitats.

The use of energy normally entails environmental costs to the soil. One example of it's impact is found within the exploration of fossil fuels. They often lie deep within the earth or under the ocean floor. To get to solid veins of the highest quality low-sulfur anthracite coal, deep mine shafts must be excavated; but they are costly and dangerous and produce vast quantities of waste rock for a now scarce resource (less than 2 percent of U.S. coal reserves). The remaining stocks of coal mostly are shallow deposits, and so the prospect is that deep mining will disappear in favor of strip mining, which requires no excavation; the overlying rock (called the overburden) is removed entirely, and the exposed coal then may be broken up and removed. Stripping is cheaper and is likely to be used even more widely when low quality coal deposits can be used more extensively. Stripping is ugly, however. It chews up landscapes, leaving big pits and mountains of overburden, and it disrupts water tables. Recently, an effective federal bill to stop "cut and run" stripping was passed, and it should help prevent the worst abuses and even correct some of the old ones in Appalachia. Most important, from now on, strip miners would be expected to restore the "approximate original contours of the landscape" before they abandon a site. Perhaps this is the first step in a world wide campaign to correct the potentially dangerous pollutants to which we have subjected our natural systems.

Test your knowledge of competency 10.

1. Which of the following events are not likely to cause changes in the water systems?
   a. runoff from a sewage plant
   b. mercury
   c. biodegradable detergents
   d. heated water from nuclear plants

2. What pollutant is primarily blamed for the excessive air pollution of today?
   a. acid rains
   b. exhaust from internal combustion engine
   c. smokestacks
   d. cigarette smoking

3. Which of the following is not a characteristic of "strip mining"?
   a. leaves the overlying rock (overburden) intact
   b. chews up landscapes
   c. disrupts water tables
   d. exposes coal to be broken up

Answers: 1. c, 2. c, 3. a

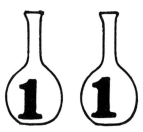

Competency 11:   Relate the structure of atoms and molecules to the characteristic behavior of matter.

Matter is composed of molecules. A molecule is the smallest particle that retains the identity of a substance. Molecules occur in various and different sizes. There is space between molecules. They are always moving rapidly, hitting other molecules and then bouncing off in different directions. All molecules attract each other. Cohesion is the attraction between molecules of the same substance. Adhesion is the attraction between molecules of different substances.

Cohesion makes possible the formation of the three physical states of matter.

In a solid, the attraction between molecules is very strong, which permits the solid to hold its shape. But the molecules have energy and vibrate in place. Wood, iron, and glass are examples of solids.

In a liquid, the attraction between molecules is much weaker. The liquid does not hold its shape, but takes the shape of the container. Water, milk, and alcohol are examples of liquids.

In a gas, there is practically no attraction between molecules, thus allowing the molecules to move away from each other and spread throughout the container. The molecules of a gas fly about at high speed but collide constantly. After each collision, they spring apart and fly on to the next collision. Air, oxygen, and carbon dioxide are examples of gases.

Adhesion makes it possible for two different substances to stick together. Paint sticks to wood because of the attraction between molecules of different materials. Adhesion causes water to stick to other substances, making them wet. The action of glue, cement, and paste also depends upon adhesion.

Molecules are made up of smaller particles called atoms. A molecule may be made of one atom or of two or more atoms. Scientists have found that atoms are made up of three smaller kinds of particles which they called electrons, protons, and neutrons.

The electron is a particle with a negative electrical charge. Electrons move about very quickly and repel each other.

The proton is a particle with a positive electrical charge. The proton is heavier than the electron, so it moves about more slowly. The electron and proton attract each other because of the unlike charges. When put together, they neutralize each other.

The neutron is a particle that has a neutral charge. It does not repel or attract other neutrons. A neutron seems to be made of one electron and one proton. The protons and neutrons, being heavier than electrons, are closely packed together in the center of the atoms. This is called the nucleus.

All atoms are made up of electrons, protons, and neutrons, but all atoms are not alike. Atoms are different because of the different numbers of electrons, protons, and neutrons they have. Each different kind of atom is called an element. The atoms of one kind of element are exactly the same, but differ from the atoms of another kind of element. Chemists define an element as a simple substance that cannot be broken up into anything simpler by ordinary chemical reactions.

There are three main classes of matter. These are elements, compounds, and mixtures. There are only 92 natural elements on earth, so most substances are either compounds or mixtures. A compound is a combination of two or more elements so that each element has lost its own special physical and chemical properties. A chemical change takes place when a compound is formed, with energy being either given off or required.

Because every compound has its own special properties, it is possible to tell one compound from another. A compound is always made up of the same elements. The number of atoms of each element that combine to form a molecule of the compound is always the same. The elements in a compound are not easily separated and require some form of energy, such as electricity or heat to cause the separation.

Another combination of elements or compounds is a mixture. In a mixture the combination of substances has not lost its own special physical and chemical properties. No new substance has been formed and does not require or give off energy. The amounts of the different materials in a mixture are not fixed and may change from time to time. They are usually easily separated.

A solution is another kind of mixture. In a solution the molecules of one substance are spread out evenly and equally between the molecules of the other substance. This is called dissolving. The substance that dissolves is the solute. It may be either a solid, liquid, or gas. The material that does the dissolving is the solvent. It is usually a liquid but may be a gas or solid. An example of a solution is sugar and water.

86

When substances are combined in a chemical change, it seems as if new matter has been created. In other chemical changes, it seems that matter is destroyed, such as burning. The Law of Conservation states that, in ordinary chemical reactions, matter is neither created nor destroyed, but only changed from one form to another. An example is burning. Gases are formed and ashes are left behind. When the wood and the air that is used to burn the wood is weighed, it is found to be the same as the weight of the ashes and the gases formed. Matter can change from one form to another, but the amount itself does not change.

Test your knowledge of competency 11.

1. The force that causes glue to hold two pieces of paper together is called
   a. cohesion
   b. magnetism
   c. adhesion
   d. mixture

2. The nucleus of the atom is made up of
   a. electrons
   b. neutrons and electrons
   c. protons, electrons, and neutrons
   d. protons and neutrons

3. A combination of elements in which a chemical change takes place is called a
   a. mixture
   b. compound
   c. solution
   d. reaction

4. The Law of Conservation states that, in ordinary chemical reactions,
   a. the amount of matter is reduced
   b. new matter can be created
   c. matter is neither created nor destroyed, but only changed
   d. matter is destroyed

Answers: 1. c, 2. d, 3. b, 4. c

Competency 12-1: Distinguish among the molecular structure of elements, compounds, and mixtures.

Matter which takes up space, or occupies space, and has weight, is made up of several substances.

The molecule is one of the basic units of matter. It is the smallest particle into which a substance can be divided and still have properties of the original substance.

Molecules are made up of simpler particles of matter called atoms. Atoms combine in various ways to form molecules. Molecules are in rapid and ceaseless motion. They attract each other.

Every kind of matter can be classified as being either an element, a compound, or a mixture.

Element

An element is a component of matter and is composed entirely of atoms of one kind. Each element has the general properties of matter and have special properties by which it can be identified.

Some things you may use everyday are elements, such as iron, tin, oxygen, and aluminum. Only a few elements are found as pure elements, such as gold and copper. Only 92 elements are known to occur naturally on the earth. All other known elements have been created in laboratories.

List of Common Elements

1. carbon	6. chlorine	11. copper
2. iron	7. sodium	12. calcium
3. neon	8. lead	13. mercury
4. oxygen	9. nickel	14. sulfur
5. tin	10. hydrogen	

Compound

A compound is a component of matter, and the molecules of a compound are made up of more than one kind of atom. A compound is made up of 2 or more different elements.

There are several thousand known compounds. An example of a compound is water--it can be changed into 2 other substances. Since this is so, water must be made up of at least 2 kinds of atoms. Other examples: salt, sugar, baking soda, glue, and gasoline.

Mixture

In a mixture, 2 or more kinds of matter are mixed together. The kinds of matter are not combined but are mixed. A simple example: mix cereal, fruit and milk in a bowl.

In some mixtures you can see the different kinds of matter; others you cannot.

On the left is shown 1 molecule of the compound carbon dioxide (CO_2). It is composed of 2 atoms of oxygen and 1 atom of carbon. The electrical valance of the carbon atom is +4 and the electrical valance of the 2 oxygen atoms is -2 for each. Carbon has 4 electrons in its outer shell and when it takes on the 4 electrons from the oxygen atoms it completes its outer shell, thus forming the compound carbon dioxide.

On the right is shown 1 molecule of water (H_2O). It is composed of 2 atoms of hydrogen and 1 atom of oxygen. The electrical valance of hydrogen is +1 for each atom which makes a total of +2 for the 2 atoms. The valance of the oxygen atom is -2. In a molecule the positive and negative charges must be equal. In a chemical equation this must also be true. Observe the chemical reaction of hydrogen and oxygen uniting to form water.

$$H_2 + O_2 \longrightarrow H_2O$$

But there are 2 atoms of oxygen on the left and only one on the right. There must be the same on both sides. So, we place a 2 in front of the water molecule.

$$H_2 + O_2 \longrightarrow 2H_2O$$

Now we must place a 2 in front of the hygrogen molecule.

$$2H_2 + O_2 \longrightarrow 2H_2O$$

Now we have that 2 molecules of hydrogen and 1 molecule of oxygen join to make 2 molecules of water. The atoms are balanced on both sides of the equation and so are the electrical charges.

90

Test your knowledge of competency 12-1.

1. A component of matter composed entirely of
    atoms of one kind.
    a. mixture
    b. element
    c. compound
    d. substance

2. The molecules of this component of matter are
    made up of more than one kind of atom.
    a. compound
    b. element
    c. iron
    d. mixture

3. A component of matter that mixes together two
    or more kinds of matter.
    a. substance
    b. mixture
    c. compound
    d. copper

Answers: 1. b, 2. a, 3. b

    Competency 12-2: Distinguish among the
molecular structure of elements, compounds, and
mixtures.

    Trees, grass, rocks, people, and nearly every-
thing in our environment is composed of molecules.
Molecules, in turn, are formed by the joining
together of atoms. All the substances that make
up matter can be divided into three main classes:
elements, compounds, and mixtures.

    Elements are often called the building blocks
of matter. Chemists also define an element as a
simple substance that cannot be broken up into
anything simpler by ordinary chemical reactions.
The simplest building block of an element is
called an atom. If the atom is somehow torn apart
or changes the number of its particles, it is no

91

longer an atom of the same element. All of the atoms of an element have the same number of protons and electrons.

When substances are mixed together without any chemical reaction (heat, light, color change, etc.) the result is called a mixture. A mixture is a substance made up of two or more elements or compounds that have combined in such a way that each element or compound has not lost its own special physical and chemical properties. The constituent parts of a mixture retain their own properties and may be separated by physical means. Examples are salt and pepper or flour and soda.

When a chemical reaction takes place between two or more substances, a compound is formed. The basic building block of the compound is the molecule. Every compound has its own special properties, and in this way it is possible for us to tell one compound from another. For example, the union of hydrogen and oxygen forms a water molecule. The union of oxygen and iron forms iron oxide or rust.

There are 92 natural elements on earth, most substances are either compounds or mixtures. Man has made 13 elements, bringing the total number to 105 elements.

	Element	Mixture	Compound
Description	Made of one kind of atom	Two or more sub-stances, chemically uncom-bined	Made of two or more kinds of atoms chemically combined
Basic Unit	Atom	Atom or Molecule	Molecule
Comment	All pieces look the same when subdivided.	May be separated into two or more substances by mechanical means.	May be separated into elements only by chemical means.

Test your knowledge of competency 12-2.

1. The basic building block of a compound is the
    _____.
    a. atom
    b. element
    c. molecule
    d. none of the above

2. A substance made up of two or more elements
    or compounds that have combined in such a way
    that each element or compound has not lost
    its own special physical and chemical pro-
    perties is called _____.
    a. a mixture
    b. an atom
    c. a proton
    d. a molecule

3. An element is made up of _____.
    a. two or more kinds of atoms chemically com-
        bined
    b. one kind of atom
    c. two or more substances, chemically uncom-
        bined
    d. one kind of electron

4. Elements, both natural and man made, total
    a. 92
    b. 102
    c. 100
    d. 105

Answers: 1. c, 2. a, 3. b, 4. d

Competency 13-1: Identify physical phases of matter. For example: identify gases, liquids, and solids; identify changes in the states of matter (i.e., evaporation).

Matter is anything that takes up, or occupies space and has weight. Matter exists in millions of forms. Most of these forms may be in three states--gases, liquids, and solids.

In the gaseous state, matter doesn't have a definite size or a definite shape. When a gas is poured into a container, it spreads out until it has the same size and shape of the container. Molecules in a gas fly about at very high speed colliding constantly.

A liquid has a definite size, but it does not have a definite shape. A liquid's shape depends upon the shape of the container. The molecules in a liquid hold loosely together but move about.

A solid has a definite size and shape. Solids can be hard or soft. The molecules in a solid stay in place, therefore, the solid holds its shape.

Evaporation is a term used by scientists to mean something dries up or when one state of matter changes to another state. When heated or cooled, matter can be changed from one state to another.

For example, when a liquid is frozen it becomes a solid; or, when liquid water is heated until it boils, it becomes a gas called steam.

Test your knowledge of competency 13-1.

1. The state of matter that has a definite size
    and shape is a
    a. gas
    b. solid
    c. substance
    d. liquid

2. Water, milk, alcohol, and gasoline are
    examples of
    a. solids
    b. liquids
    c. gases
    d. both c and b

Answers: 1. b, 2. b

Competency 13-2: Identify physical phases of
matter. Identify changes in the state of matter.

Matter is anything that takes up, or occupies,
space and has weight. All materials about us consist of matter. Some kinds of matter are easily
observed such as a stone or a piece of wood.
Other kinds of matter are recognized less readily,
such as the air.

Matter is found in three forms or states and
these states are called solid, liquid and gas.

A solid has both a definite volume and a
definite shape. Solids can be hard or soft. A
solid does not need lateral support to prevent it
from losing its shape. A block of wood placed on
a table keeps its shape and its volume.

A liquid has a definite volume, but it does
not have a definite shape. A liquid takes the
shape of its container. We find that a liquid has
a definite volume if we try to put a quart of milk

96

into a pint bottle. A liquid must have lateral support to retain its shape.

Gas has neither a definite shape nor a definite volume. This fact makes it difficult to measure the volume of gas. When a gas is poured into a container it spreads out until it has the same size of the container, and also takes the shape of the container. A pint of air would expand and occupy all that space if it were placed in a really empty quart bottle.

Physical changes are those in which the identifying properties of substances remain unchanged. Ice melts, water boils, liquid freezes, glass breaks, and sugar dissolves in water. In all these cases matter undergoes some change. Its form may be different or it may have experienced a change of state of energy level. However, in no case has the matter lost its identity. Sometimes by a reversal of the action which caused the change, the material may be restored to its original form and the same identifying properties are again readily recognized. In such changes only the alterations in physical properties are apparent; the composition of the material is not changed.

Freezing, melting, evaporation and condensation are physical changes.

(a) Freezing - To pass from the liquid to the solid state by loss of heat.

(b) Melting - To be changed from a solid state to a liquid state by the application of heat, pressure, or both.

(c) Evaporation - When water changes from a liquid into an invisible gas.

(d) Condensation - When water vapor changes into a liquid.

Chemical changes are those in which new substances with new properties are formed. Examples of chemical changes are the burning of wood, rusting of iron, tarnishing of silver, souring of milk, plants decay and digestion of food. For a chemical change to take place, energy such as heat, light or electricity is either needed or given off.

Test your knowledge of competency 13-2.

1. Of the following, the one which represents the conversion of a liquid to a gas is
    a. evaporation
    b. oxidation
    c. condensation
    d. sublimation

2. Which of the following changes are physical?
    a. burning coal and tarnishing silver
    b. magnetizing steel and exploding gunpowder
    c. boiling water and melting shortening
    d. none of the above

Answers: 1. a, 2. c

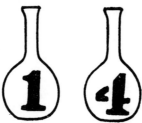

Competency 14: Describe the role of chemical reaction in relation to living organisms.

A chemical reaction is any process that causes a chemical change in one or more substances. Chemist describe chemical reactions in terms of combinations or separation of atoms and groups of atoms. Countless numbers of atoms take part in all chemical reactions that occur in nature or in the laboratory.

Living organisms are effected by such physical reactions as freezing, boiling, or dissolving. These physical reactions do not alter the structure of the atom. Chemical reactions create a change in the configuration of the atom.

There are chemical reactions going on all around us all the time. No living organism is excluded from chemical reactions. The digestion of food the organism eats is a chemical reaction.

Many of the chemical reactions are very good and are essential for a living organism. Others destroy living things. An ecologist is concerned with preserving the balance of nature. An ecologist investigates the interactions of organisms in various kinds of environments.

Ecology shows that man cannot regard nature as separate and detached--something to look at on a visit to a forest or a drive through the country. Any change man makes in his environment affects all the organisms in it. When cars and factories pollute the air, animals and plants, as well as man himself is harmed.

Chemical reactions such as water polluted by chemicals and waste threatens remote streams and lakes.

Each kind of life is suited to the physical conditions of its habitat--the type of soil, the amount of moisture and light, the quality of air, the annual variations in temperature. Each survives because of chemical reactions such as changing air and food into blood. However, if chemical reactions are introduced into the living organisms life, its existence may be threatened and its balance is disturbed.

Natural balances are disrupted when crops are planted in a region, fertilized, and sprayed with pesticides.

Living organisms are classified as producers, consumers, and decomposers. Not one of these could exist without chemical reactions. Green plants of any kind, whether stately oaks or tiny algae, are producers because they make their own food through photosynthesis. Animals, including man, feed on plants or on other animals and are therefore called consumers. Organisms that cause decay, such as bacteria and fungi, are decomposers.

Chemical reactions play a very important role in relation to all living organisms.

Test your knowledge of competency 14.

1. A chemical reaction is any process that
    causes a/an _____.
    a. physical change
    b. chain reaction
    c. chemical change
    d. atomic imbalance

2. _____ is/are chemical reactions.
   a. digestion of food
   b. photosynthesis
   c. burning paper
   d. all of the above

Answers: 1. c, 2. d

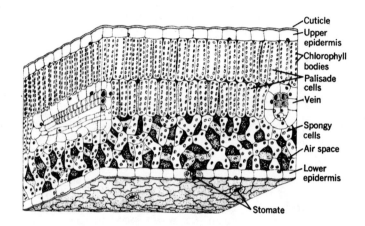

THE FOOD FACTORY OF THE PLANT
A SECTION OF A LEAF

The scientific name for the process of sugar-making is made of two words that emphasize the key aspect of the action. Photo means light; synthesis means putting together. Photosynthesis means putting together by means of light, this is exactly what happens in the process.

The plant cells can change the sugar into starch for storage or combine it with other materials to build substances such as proteins and vitamins. Sugar can also be converted into fats. The sugar-making process in green plants produces the primary material of all foodstuffs.

Competency 15: Define the basic concepts of physics (mass, length, gravity, energy, weight).

Physics is the science concerned with matter and energy. There are three basic principles of physics; mass, linear and angular momentum, potential and kinetic energy.

Mass is defined in terms of the force that is needed to overcome or change a body's inertia. The mass of a body is a measure of its inertia. A body will stay at rest, or it will stay in motion if it's in motion. This is the principle of inertia. An outside force is needed to change an object's inertia. The greater a body's mass, the more force it will need to overcome its inertia. More force is required to move an automobile than a ping pong ball. And, more force will be needed to stop an automobile than a ping pong ball.

Force is simply the push or the pull on the mass of an object. An object's length, its linear construction, is a matter of how long it happens to be. A body's weight is defined as the measure of the earth's pull of gravity on the body.

Every body attracts or pulls on every other body, and this attraction is called gravity. The larger and heavier an object is, the greater its pull. The farther away the object is, the smaller is the pull. The earth's gravity pulls a body down toward the center. This keeps us from falling off the earth, and it holds the air and water on the earth.

The earth sustains two basic forms of energy--
kinetic energy and potential energy.

Energy is defined as the ability of matter to
move other matter or to produce a chemical change
in other matter. Scientists sometimes define
energy as the ability to do work.

Kinetic energy is the energy a body has
because it's in motion--it's moving.

Potential energy is the energy a body has due
to its position or condition--its stored-up energy.
A rock held over another object, water closed
inside a dam, a stretched rubber band, a wound-up
spring, chemicals in a dry cell, gunpowder--all
represent potential energy. When their potential
energy is set free, it becomes kinetic energy
because it's in motion. Releasing of the rubber
band, letting go of the rock, exploding the gun-
powder, changes the potential energy into kinetic
energy.

The law of conservation of mass and energy
states that no matter what forms that mass and
energy take their sum is always constant. Under
special circumstances, mass can be converted into
energy, as with the atomic bomb through Einstein's
efforts.

There is also the conservation principle of
linear and angular momentum. Linear momentum is
an object of mass moving fast in a straight line.
The momentum is constant unless it's acted upon by
an outside force. The greater the weight and
speed of the moving object, the more difficult it
is for an outside force to stop it. With angular
momentum, the object is rotating, like a top spin-
ning or a wheel turning. A rotating object has
rotational kinetic energy in addition to its
kinetic energy as a result of its linear motion as
well.

According to the law of conservation of energy,

energy is not created nor is it destroyed--it's only changed from one form to another.

Test your knowledge of competency 15.

1. The area of physics concerned with an object's stored-up energy is
    a. mass
    b. potential energy
    c. kinetic energy
    d. weight

2. The measure of the earth's pull of gravity on a body is
    a. mass
    b. weight
    c. length
    d. inertia

Answers: 1. b, 2. b

Competency 16: Define types of energy (e.g., identify electrical, chemical, nuclear, heat, light, mechanical, solar energy).

Energy is the ability of matter to move other matter or to produce a chemical change in other matter.

Electrical energy is the energy produced by electrons moving through a substance. A stream of these electrons moving through a substance is called an electric current. Electrical energy runs motors, lights our homes, and makes our telephones, radios, and television sets operate.

Chemical energy is a form of potential energy because the energy is stored in substances. Chemical energy is released when a chemical reaction occurs and new substances are formed. These new substances are formed because of the action between the electrons in the outermost shells or energy levels in atoms of different substances.

Nuclear energy comes from the nucleus of an atom when one atom splits and becomes two. Nuclear energy also comes when the nuclei of atoms are fused together. There is a large amount of energy released in each case.

Heat energy is the energy produced by the moving molecules in a substance. The faster the molecules move, the more heat energy a substance has, and the hotter it becomes. Heat energy dries our clothes, cooks our food, heats our homes, and runs power plants.

The form of energy that we most often see around us is mechanical energy. The energy that is produced from machines is mechanical energy. Also, all moving bodies produce mechanical energy.

Solar energy is the form of energy that comes from the sun. A great deal of attention is now being given to solar energy and many experts agree that it is the energy of the future because the sun will last forever. Today, some homes and businesses use solar energy to power their heating systems and water heaters. However, much research and experimentation remains to be done in the area of solar energy.

Light energy is energy provided by rays of the sun. This visible light provides energy for plants and animals to maintain life on earth. Without it, there would be no life as we know it on earth.

Test your knowledge of competency 16.

1. Energy that is produced by moving molecules in a substance is called
   a. light energy
   b. nuclear energy
   c. heat energy
   d. electrical energy

2. The form of energy that we most often see around us is
   a. solar energy
   b. mechanical energy
   c. nuclear energy
   d. chemical energy

3. Which of the following is not a type of energy?
   a. solar
   b. light
   c. chemical
   d. stored
   e. electrical

Answers: 1. c, 2. b, 3. d

Competency 17: Analyze the physical properties of matter (e.g., identify the characteristics
of matter; solids, liquids, and gases; elasticity
of matter; simple harmonic motions; fluids at rest;
and fluids in motion).

Matter is anything that takes up space and
has weight. All matter is made up of molecules.
Matter is found in three states: solids, liquids,
and gases. The states of matter act differently
because of the movement of their molecules.

Solids have a definite size and shape. They
can be hard or soft. The attraction between the
molecules is very strong, so the solid holds its
shape. Examples of solids are wood, ice, iron,
and plastic.

Liquids have a definite size, but it does not
have a definite shape. A liquid's shape depends
upon the shape of the container into which it is
poured. The attraction of molecules is much weaker
than in a solid and although the molecules still
stick together it will not hold its own shape.
Examples of liquids are water, oil, milk and tea.

Gases do not have either a definite size or a
definite shape. When gas is poured into a container, it spreads out until it has the same size
and the same shape of the container. The molecules
have very little attraction for each other, so
they spread throughout the container holding it.
Examples of gases are oxygen, carbon dioxide,
nitrogen and air.

The physical properties of matter include
such characteristics as color, odor, taste,
heaviness, hardness, brittleness, elasticity,
melting and boiling temperatures, solubility in
water and other liquids, conductivity of heat and
electricity, ductility, and malleability.

Matter sometimes changes state. A change of
state takes place during melting, boiling, evaporation, and freezing.

A physical change takes place when matter
changes, but the molecules do not change. Changes
in state, size, shape, and color are physical
changes.

Elasticity is a characteristic of matter
which allows a change in the shape caused by a
force to return to its original shape when the
force is removed. Examples of matter with
elasticity are a rubber band, a spring, and a bow
that bends back to its original shape after the
string is released.

Matter at rest tends to stay at rest; matter
in motion tends to remain in motion at a constant
speed along a straight-line path. Matter will
change their states of motion only in the presence
of a net force. Movement of liquids continue
until forced to stop by another force, such as
water in a pan. Liquids at rest will stay at rest
until another force causes it to move.

Simple harmonic motion is the most important
type of periodic motion, movement that tends to
repeat itself at regular intervals. It is
illustrated by a weight bobbing up and down at the
end of a spiral spring, or, approximately, by a
swinging pendulum.

Fluids and Solids

1. Principles of Fluid Mechanics

> Little drops of water
> Little grains of sand
> Make the mighty ocean
> And the pleasant land.
>
> R. L. Stevenson
> A Child's Garden of Verses

Fluids and solids appear everywhere in nature. There is an essential similarity between fluids and solids. A few simple physical laws can be applied to explain a wide variety of natural phenomena.

Fluid mechanics is not limited in its applications to discussing things like the flow of fluids in laboratories or the motion of tides on the earth, but it can successfully be applied to systems as different as the atomic nucleus on the one hand, and the galaxy on the other. In dealing with a fluid we are dealing with a system which has many particles which interact with each other. The main utility of fluid mechanics is the ability to develop a formalism which deals solely with a few macroscopic quantities like pressure, ignoring the details of the particle interactions, the techniques of fluid mechanics have often been found useful in making models of systems with complicated structure where interactions take place between the constituents. The first successful model of the fission of heavy elements was the liquid drop model of the nucleus, which treats the nucleus as a fluid, and thus replaces the problem of calculating the interactions of all of the protons and neutrons with the much simpler problem of calculating the pressures and surface tensions in a fluid. This treatment gives only a rough approximation to reality, but it is nonetheless a useful way of approaching the problem.

A classical fluid is defined as a medium which is infinitely divisible. Our knowledge of atomic physics tell us that real fluids are made up of atoms and molecules, and that if we go to small enough scale, the structure of a fluid will not be continuous. Nevertheless, the classical picture will be approximately correct provided that we do not look at the fluid in too fine a detail. For example, when we introduce "infinitesimal" volume elements of the fluid, we do not mean to imply that the volume really tends to zero, but merely that the volume element is very small compared to the overall dimensions of the fluid, but very large compared to the dimensions of the constituent atoms or molecules.

The basic laws of fluid motion follow from some very simple physical principles. These principles are (1) matter can neither be created nor destroyed and (2) Newton's second law of motion (F = ma, the net unbalanced force producing a change of motion is equal to the product of the mass and the acceleration of the particle).

2.   Fluids in Astrophysics

There are more things in heaven and earth, Horatio, Than are dreamt of in your philosophy.

> William Shakespeare
> Hamlet, Act I, Scene V

Astrophysics is the science of the physical properties and phenomena of the stars, planets, etc.

The earth can be treated as a fluid mass. Suppose we want to know how realistic such an approximation could be. One measure would be to calculate its rotational frequency and compare it with the actual frequency of rotation. These two agree to about 20%, so that if we can be satisfied with that sort of accuracy, we can indeed treat the earth as a fluid mass (even though we know it to be solid).

By going to a frame rotating with a fluid
mass, the dynamical problem of calculating the
motion of such fluids can be replaced by the
static problem of balancing pressure, centrifugal
force, and gravitation. The method of calculating
equilibrium shapes for such bodies is quite simple
in principle (although sometimes complicated
mathematically). We simply calculate the gravitational potential for the body, insert this into
the Euler equation, and demand that a surface of
constant pressure coincide with the surface of a
body. In this way, various physical systems can
be examined, including ellipsoids (such as the
earth), disks (such as the galaxy), and rings
(such as those around Saturn), and it is possible
to find equilibrium configurations for each shape.

3.   The Idea of Stability

Bright star, were I as steadfast as thou art!

John Keats
Sonnet written on a blank
page in Shakespeare's
poems

For a system to be in stable equilibrium, we
must not only have a situation in which forces are
in balance, but where small deviations of the
system from the equilibrium must generate forces
which tend to drive the system back toward its
equilibrium configuration, rather than farther
away from it. The classic example of such a system
is a mass on the end of an unstretched spring.
Any movement of the mass away from this equilibrium
position results in the spring exerting a force
pulling or pushing the mass back toward its
original position.

A ball sitting on top of a hill is an example
of an unstable equilibrium, since small changes of
position would result in the ball being driven

farther and farther from equilibrium. A third
type of equilibrium, neutral equilibrium, can be
defined between these two. This is a situation in
which movement away from the equilibrium position
results in no forces being exerted at all. A ball
on a flat table top would be an example of such a
system.

The general requirement that a system be in a
stable equilibrium is that every possible perturbation of the system leads to a state of higher
total energy. It is always possible that a system
could be stable against one type of perturbation,
but unstable against another.

4.   Fluids in Motion

No man steps into the same river twice.

Heraclitus

The first thing we have to decide is how to
characterize the motion of a fluid. If we think
of a fluid as being composed of infinitesimal
volume elements, then a volume element located at
coordinates (x, y, z) will have some velocity
v(x, y, z, t).

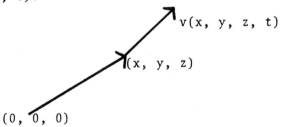

This means that to each point in space we can
assign a vector which can be, in general, a function of both position and time. This collection
of velocities is referred to as a velocity field.

If a perturbation, once introduced, grows
with time, the fluid system is said to be unstable.

112

5. Waves in Fluids

What dreadful noise of waters in mine ears!

William Shakespeare
King Richard III, Act I,
Scene IV

In general, we can think of wave motion as the result of two opposing forces acting on a body. Consider a weight on a spring. If a force is applied which moves the weight away from its equilibrium position, the weight will exert a force which pulls the weight back. If we let go, the spring will return to its equilibrium position, but when it gets there, it will be moving with some velocity. Thus it will overshoot the equilibrium position, and move on until the spring is compressed enough to cause it to reverse its direction. Thus, the existence of the restoring force in the spring leads to the familiar simple harmonic motion.

The situation with fluids is quite similar. Consider a body of uniform fluid whose height is unperturbed, but whose surface is for some reason perturbed. This fluid is in a gravitational field on the surface of the earth, the fluid elements in the surface will be pulled downward by gravity, while the fluid pressure will tend to exert an upward force. Thus, we might expect to see harmonic motion in this system.

There are a wide variety of waves possible in fluids. These include long waves, in which the vertical motion of the fluid can be ignored so long as the depth of the fluid is much less than the wavelength; surface waves, in which the disturbance of the wave diminishes with depth in the fluid, and capillary waves, which depend on the existence of surface tension, and are typically of short wavelength. This does not exhaust the number of possible waves in fluids, but represents the types of waves most commonly encountered in physical situations.

6.   Tides

> A ring from his finger he hastily drew
> Saying, "Take it, dearest Nellie, that your
>   heart may be true.
> For the good ship stands waiting for the
>   next flowing tide
> And if ever I return again, I will make
>   you my bride."

Traditional English
Ballad

The net gravitational attraction at the surface of the moon is given by the disturbing potential. This attraction is the cause of the tides (considered long waves). Tides at an arbitrary point will be of three types--a monthly tide, a daily tide, and a semi-diurnal tide (twice a day). For some simple forms of the depth law for the oceans, it is possible to solve for these tides explicitly, taking into account the rotation of the earth. The semi-diurnal tides are the most important.

7.   Oscillations of Fluid Spheres: Vibrations of the Earth and Nuclear Fission

He felt the earth move out and away from under them.

Ernest Hemingway
For Whom the Bell Tolls

For some purposes it is reasonable to treat the earth as if it were a uniform liquid. If we ignore the rotation of the earth, then the equilibrium configuration of the earth would be a sphere. If the earth were slightly deformed (e.g., by an earthquake) and then allowed to respond, what could be expected to happen? The liquid sphere (earth) would perform oscillations about its equilibrium configuration. This phenomenon is similar to the ringing of a bell and has recently been measured by geophysicists.

The Liquid Drop Model of the Nucleus

It may seem strange that the classical theory of fluids should have anything to do with nuclear effects, but actually it is not. The problem of describing a nucleus made up of many interacting nucleons is in many ways similar to the problem of describing a gas made up of many interacting particles. If one does not want to get involved in the impossible problem of describing the motion of each particle in detail, one treats the system as an ensemble, and discusses only the gross properties, ignoring the detailed structure as much as possible. In the case of liquid one can use fluid mechanics. Since a fluid is the simplest system in which this averaging process can be done, it is natural to try to approximate any system with a complex internal structure by a fluid. The liquid drop model represents such a zero-order approximation to the behavior of large nuclei. In the topic of surface tension, the existence of an attractive force between the constituent particles of a liquid give rise to a surface force. A nucleus is made up of protons and neutrons, so that if there were no force present other than electromagnetic ones, the nucleus would have to fly apart because of the repulsion between protons. The existence of nuclei is true evidence for the existence of short-range attractive forces between the nucleons. These are the strong interactions which constitute one of the major fields of investigation in modern physics. Such a force would give rise to a surface tension in the nuclear "fluid." The stability of the nucleus is thus seen to be a result of the competition between the electrostatic forces, which tend to blow the nucleus apart, and the strong interactions giving rise to a surface tension, which tends to hold the nucleus together. These two forces play similar roles to gravity and centrifugal force, whose competition is the main point of investigation in the study of stars.

Nuclear Fission

Although the use of the fission process in reactors has been widespread, the problem of the fission of heavy elements has, until very recently, defied theoretical analysis. The liquid drop model of the nucleus can be used to come to some qualitative understanding of how energy can be derived from fission.

The liquid drop model predicts that when a nucleus breaks up, it should split into two equal-sized fragments. Remember that any nucleus can be split. This is not the case. When uranium undergoes fission, the end products are clustered so that one fragment is around 90, the other is around 140. This is one of the main difficulties of the liquid drop model--one of its failures. The question of why nuclei should go to unequal fragments has been the subject of a long investigation in the theory of heavy nuclei.

We can still use the model, however, because although it is wrong in some details, it nevertheless reproduces the general features of nuclear structure quite well in a simple way.

Most of the current research on fission has to do with mapping out the complicated energy surfaces which correspond to various deformations of the nucleus, and then trying to decide how fission will proceed for real nuclei.

Induced fission is the basic principle by which a fission reactor works. If the nucleus in question is U_{235} (a type of uranium), then a neutron striking the nucleus can supply the energy needed to put the nucleus over the top of the potential barrier and energy is released. Since some of this energy is released in the form of neutrons, which can, in turn, initiate further reactions, it is possible to sustain a continuous

116

fission process from which energy is extracted.

The behavior of the system close to equilibrium need not be related simply to the behavior of the system far from equilibrium. This aspect of the physical world is only beginning to be explored, and very little is known about it at present.

In conclusion we can state: First, a fluid such as the earth acting under the influence of its own gravity will execute periodic vibrations about equilibrium if deformed and then released; second, a charged fluid under the influence of surface tension such as a nucleus will fission spontaneously for certain values of the charge (the process of nuclear fission).

8.   Viscosity in Fluids

Slow as molasses in January.

Southern Folk Saying

In an ideal fluid, the only way in which a force can be generated or, equivalently, in which momentum can be transferred, is through the pressure gradient. On the atomic level this corresponds to collisions in which the momentum of a molecule in the direction of the force is reversed. A force of this type must always be normal to the surface on which it is being exerted. In addition, if we were somehow able to reach into an ideal fluid and apply a force to a single fluid element, there would be nothing other than pressure gradients to oppose the motion of the element, so that it could be quickly accelerated.

To see the shortcomings of this description of a fluid, consider the following example: Let there be a fluid of depth h which is not moving. Let another layer of identical fluid be flowing across the top of the stationary layer at a velocity v. For a classical ideal fluid, the

fluid in the upper layer will keep moving indefi-
nitely, even if no forces are acting on it.
However, in a real situation, the top layer would
eventually slow down and stop. This means that
there must be some way of exerting forces which
are different from the pressure, and act along a
surface, rather than normal to it.

The term usually used to describe such a
situation is that the fluid is capable of exerting
a "shear force", in addition to the pressure. The
phenomenon associated with this force is called
"viscosity".

9.   Heat, Thermal Connection, and the Circulation
      of the Atmosphere

            For I had done a dreadful thing
            And it would work us woe
            For all averred I'd killed the bird
            That made the breeze to blow

                        Samuel Taylor Coleridge
                        Rime of the Ancient
                              Mariner

On the atomic scale, we are used to thinking
of temperature as being associated with the motions
of atoms. If the atoms have a large kinetic
energy, we speak of a high temperature. Similarly,
we define absolute zero classically as the temperature at which the kinetic energy vanishes. Consider what would happen if we had a fluid in which
one part was heated to a temperature higher than
its neighbors. In the heated section, the molecules would be moving faster. In the course of
their collisions with surrounding molecules, some
of this energy would, on the average, be transferred to molecules which were originally moving
more slowly, thereby speeding them up. Observing
this, we would say that heat was being transferred
from the hot to the cold region.

When a fluid is heated in the presence of a

gravitational field, it is possible for an instability to occur, in which the warm fluid will rise and the cold fluid fall. This is called thermal convection. The general circulation of the atmosphere can be thought of as being due to the unequal heating of the earth at the poles and equator.

10. General Properties of Solids--Statics

I can be pushed just so far.

H. L. Wilson
Ruggles of Red Gap

Fluids are characterized by the fact that on the microscopic level, the atoms interact mainly by collisions. The only forces which are generated inside of a fluid mass are those having to do with the momentum transferred through these collisions. We customarily refer to such forces as pressures. If we wished to apply an external force to a particular element in the fluid, however, it is clear that, aside from possible viscous drag, there is no way to generate forces inside the fluid which would oppose the applied force. Consequently, the fluid element would be in motion for as long as the force were applied.

If we think about a solid, however, we know that this is not true. If I push on a table top, the material immediately under my hand does not move. This means that the solid, unlike the fluid, is capable of generating internal forces which can oppose forces applied from the outside. The reason for this becomes clear if we think about the crystalline structure of the atoms in most solids. The atoms are locked into their places in a crystal lattice by electromagnetic interactions with other atoms, so that in order to move one atom, it is necessary to overcome the strong forces which bind it to other atoms (which, in turn, are bound to other atoms, and so forth). It is these atomic forces which we describe

119

classically as "internally generated forces" in discussing solids, and which are absent in the case of fluids.

The question of how much and in what manner a solid will deform under an applied force is an experimental one. There is no reason to expect, a priori, any particular kind of behavior. For example, if we imagined that the internal forces between the atoms in a solid could be represented by springs, then we might expect that the deformation would be proportional to the force applied. Such a solid is called an elastic solid. We could also imagine that the forces between the atoms were such that they allowed no motion of the atoms unless the external force were strong enough to overcome them. In this case, there would be no deformation for small forces, and large deformations for large forces when, presumably, the material would fracture. Between these two extremes, one could imagine many different kinds of solids, and, indeed, there is an entire field of study called rheology, which is devoted to the study of the way in which materials react to forces applied to them.

In general, we can think of the process of the formation of mountain chains as a folding of the crust when a force is applied along the surface of the earth. This force might arise when the leading edge of a continent is pushed by continental drift against the underlying mantle. It is thought, for example, that the mountain chain on the west coast of North and South America was formed in this way. In general, a mountain chain will have the general shape shown in the drawing, where the largest mountains are closest to the applied force P, and the height of the mountains varies inversely with the distance from the force. There are, of course, exceptions to this general rule in nature, caused either by a nonuniformity in the crust or by deflections of the surface which exist before the force is applied.

The Formation of Mountain Chains

When a solid is subjected to external forces
or torques, it generates within itself forces and
torques which tend to oppose those being applied
externally, and hence to bring the entire system
into a state of static equilibrium. For the case
of an elastic solid, an equation can be written
down which relates the amount of deformation of
the solid to the magnitude of the external force.

Depending on the boundary conditions and the
forces acting, this equation can be used to
describe the general features of geological formations like lacoliths and mountain chains, or the
buckling of struts when large axial loads are
applied.

11. Nuclear Explosions

> A vast, limitless expanse of water...
> spread before us....'The Central Sea'
> sailing under
>
> Jules Verne
> <u>A Journey to the Center</u>
> <u>of the Earth</u>

Another application of the knowledge of waves
in solids is in the field of arms control. The
ability to limit the development of nuclear
weapons depends directly on the ability to detect
nuclear tests. When such tests are carried out in
the atmosphere, the detection is relatively simple,
since prevailing winds will carry radioactive
debris across national boundaries to detecting
stations. Underground tests, however, are not so

easy to detect, since the debris is confined (barring an accidental release of radioactive materials into the atmosphere). In fact, the only indication that such a test has occurred which would be detectable at large distances from the site of the test would be the seismic signal generated by the explosion. This, in turn, leads us to the question of how seismic waves are generated. (Seismic waves: waves that are characteristic of an earthquake.)

Before turning to this question, however, let us review briefly the sequence of events which follows a nuclear explosion. Immediately following the blast, tremendous pressure (on the order of 10^6 atmospheres) are present. The sudden release of energy completely strips the atoms in the neighborhood of the blast, and two things occur: (1) a burst of electromagnetic radiation moves away from the blast site, and (2) the debris of the blast moves away also, forming a shock front. At the beginning, the radiation front moves quickly, heating up the surrounding material and forming an expanding "fireball" of high temperature gases. As the fireball expands, its temperature drops and the expansion slows down. At some point, called breakaway, the shock wave overtakes the radiation front and moves ahead of it.

In atmospheric explosions, this is a complete description of the blast phenomenon. In underground explosions, however, there is another quantity which enters and that is the size of the cavity in which the explosion occurs. For the sake of simplicity, we will assume throughout the rest of this section that we are dealing with a spherically symmetric geometry. If the radius of the cavity is less than the radius at which breakaway occurs, then the fireball will actually strike the cavity walls, vaporizing them. Since more energy is required to vaporize rock than to heat up air, the fireball will be slowed down. When the shock front catches up with the fireball and moves ahead, one of two things may happen:

(1) the shock front will have sufficient energy to continue vaporizing the rock, (2) the shock front will have only enough energy to melt the surrounding rock. In either case, as the shock wave proceeds out from the blast site the damage which it does decreases. At large distances, the rock will be fractured, but it is clear that at some distance the deformation of the rock caused by the shock front will not exceed the elastic limits, and the rock will simply be deformed elastically, which means that it will exert internal forces which will bring it back to its original position. We speak of the shock wave "decaying" into an elastic wave at this point. The question which we must ask has to do with relating the deformation to the seismic wave which would be detected at large distances.

It should be obvious from the foregoing discussion that it is possible to heighten or reduce the effects of the blast by choosing the cavity radius to be greater or less than the fireball redius, and by choosing the material surrounding the blast site. Thus, a small cavity in solid rock (a "tamped" explosion) would produce much greater seismic signals than a large cavity in a very porous material. This problem, which involves the coupling of the explosion to seismic waves, is obviously of great interest to those concerned with arms control.

12. Flow of the Blood

Physics is love, engineering is marriage.

Norman Mailer
Of a Fire on the Moon

The body is a system which operates according to the same physical laws as do other natural systems. There are many parts of the body where it seems obvious that a simple physical model would explain a great deal of the observed behavior. The skeleton, for example, can be thought of as a structural system in which external loads are counteracted by internally generated forces, just as was the case for mountain chains. There are many fluid systems in the body, the most obvious of which is the circulatory system. But even at the cellular level classical processes of osmosis and diffusion through membranes are extremely important.

We shall discuss some simple models for two physical systems: The flow of blood through an artery, and the behavior of the external urine stream. The first of these is an old problem which has received a great deal of attention in the past, while the second represents a relatively new application of physical reasoning to diagnostic medicine.

The circulatory system can, with a great deal of oversimplification, be considered as shown following.

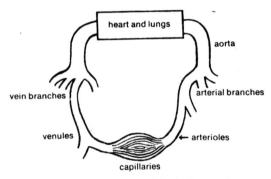

A schematic view of the circulatory system.

The blood is pumped from the heart and lungs through a system of branching arteries, whose size diminishes with distance from the heart. Eventually, it flows through the network of capillaries and back into the venous system, which returns it to the heart and lungs.

124

The basic problem of blood flow can be stated as follows: Given the time dependence of the pressure and the flow at the exit of the heart, and given the composition and layout of the arterial and venous systems, what will the flow and pressure be at any point in the body? This is an extremely complicated problem, and we are a long way from being able to describe the circulatory system mathematically. Perhaps a few remarks about the complexity of the system will help the reader to understand why.

The first problem is the nature of blood itself. Strictly speaking, it is not a fluid in the classical sense in which we have used the term up to this point, but is a suspension of small particles in a fluid (known as the plasma). The most important of these particles from the point of view of the circulation are the red blood cells, which are roughly the shape of a doughnut with the center partially filled in, and are typically about 7 microns across (1 micron = 10^{-4}cm). When we are dealing with arteries, whose dimensions are typically in the millimeter range, this is not too important an effect, but the size of a typical capillary is much smaller. This means that flow in the artery will be quite different in character from that in a capillary. In the former, the size of the vessel is very large compared to the size of the cells, so that it is reasonable to treat the blood as a classical fluid. In capillaries, however, the cells must go through one at a time (the process is similar to pushing a cork through a bottle neck). In vessels of intermediate size, like the arterioles, the problem is even more complex.

Even if we restrict our attention to the arteries, we immediately encounter difficulties which we have not run into before. We have always argued that it is a good approximation to treat liquids as incompressible, so that the equation of continuity takes on a particularly simple form. In addition, we have always been able to assume

125

that the coefficient of viscosity of a fluid, defined was a constant, independent of the motion of the fluid. Because of its peculiar composition, neither of these assumptions is true for blood. It is, in fact, a relatively compressible fluid, and its coefficient of viscosity depends markedly on the velocity. This means that the mathematical equation becomes extremely complicated even if we can treat blood as a classical fluid, and explains the relatively primitive state of the theory of blood flow.

A second important complication in the problem of blood flow is the fact that the boundary conditions are no longer of the simple form we have grown accustomed to. The walls of the arteries are not rigid, but are in fact deformable solids. Thus, when a pulse comes down the artery, the walls expand. Nor is the arterial wall necessarily of the simple type which can be described by a law for an elastic material. In fact, the arterial wall is composed of a rather complicated material whose properties under stress fall into the general class of materials called viscoelastic. This means that the response to an applied force depends on the rate at which that force is applied, as would be appropriate for a Newtonian solid, as well as the usual restoring force which is proportional to the magnitude of the applied force. In addition, at large deformations, the structure of the arterial wall itself comes into play. It is composed of two substances, elastin and collagen (a third structural component

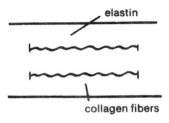

The arterial wall at rest.

126

smooth muscle, is not thought to have much effect on the elastic properties of the wall). The elastin is a rubbery, extensible material, while the collagen is more like a fiber which has a high resistance to deformation. The collagen is strung very loosely in the wall, with a lot of slack (see Figure), so that for small deformations, it has no effect on the walls. When the wall is stressed so that the slack is taken up, however, we have the situation shown following, in which the collagen now takes over and prevents further deformation of the artery. The biological usefulness of such a system is obvious, but equally obvious is the fact that such a structure is extremely difficult to describe mathematically.

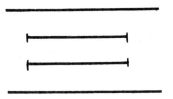

The arterial wall under tension.

Nevertheless, it is the job of the scientist to deal with complicated systems when they occur in nature. The general line of attack which is usually followed is to make a series of approximations which simplify the problem to the point where it is mathematically tractable, and then hope that the solution which is obtained has the main features of the system which we are trying to describe.

13. The Urinary Drop Spectrometer

Another, more speculative application is the urinary drop spectrometer. This is an instrument whose function is to provide early diagnoses of abnormalities in the urinary tract.

In the following figure is presented a simplified sketch of the lower urinary tract. The urine from the kidneys is stored in the bladder, and passes to the outside through a deformable tube called the urethra. Since the urethra is open to

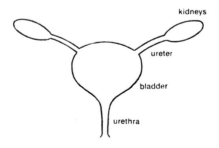

A schematic diagram of a urinary system.

the outside, it is constantly being invaded by bacteria. Urination performs the important function of washing these bacteria out.

Clearly, obstructions or impediments to the flow will give the bacteria a chance to cause infections in the urethra, which will, in turn, weaken the tissue and make the system more susceptible to infection at a later date. Over the course of years, these infections can progress to the bladder, and even the kidneys. For this reason (as well as for many others which are equally compelling), it is important to be able to develop a diagnostic technique for detecting these small obstructions and impediments before they have a chance to cause a great deal of damage.

The urinary drop spectrometer is such a technique. It works on the following principle: The stream of urine passes through the urethra during the process of urination, and flows around the obstruction. Information about the obstruction is then contained in the stream, which emerges and breaks into drops. It is a reasonable assumption that some of the information about the obstruction

128

is transmitted to these drops. If we then arrange things so that the drops interrupt a light beam between a light source and a phototube (see figure), then each drop will correspond to a pulse in the output of the tube. If we knew how to analyze this set of pulses, we would be able to gather information about the condition of the urethra from a normal urination. Such a technique, if it were perfected, would be something like a chest X-ray for the urinary system--it could be a routine part of a physical examination, and could give early warning of urinary tract difficulties.

Obviously, the hydrodynamic problems associated with the transfer of information about the obstruction to the drops are extremely difficult. Once the stream emerges from the urethra an entirely new set of considerations comes into play. We then have a cylindrical tube of fluid moving along under the influence of two forces: The pressure of the fluid and the surface tension. Such a system is called a capillary jet.

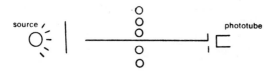

The urinary drop spectrometer.

The question of how the drops are formed, and how they can be related to urethral obstructions, is not understood at the present time.

Test your knowledge of competency 17.

1. The three states of matter are
    a. molecules, gases, and liquids
    b. solids, molecules, and liquids
    c. solids, liquids, and gases
    d. solids, gases, and molecules

2. A physical change takes place when
    a. molecules are very close together, and
        the state of matter stays the same
    b. the state of matter changes, but the
        molecules do not change
    c. the state of matter stays the same, but
        the molecules change
    d. the state of matter changes, and the
        molecules change

3. Examples of matter are
    a. basketball, chair, cup
    b. water, milk, tea
    c. air, carbon dioxide, oxygen
    d. all of the above

4. The main utility of fluid mechanics is
    a. the ability to develop a formalism which
        deals solely with a few macroscopic
        quantities like pressure
    b. ignoring the details of the particle
        interactions
    c. making models of systems with complicated
        structure
    d. a, b, and c

5. A classical fluid is defined as a medium
    which is
    a. infinitely divisible
    b. finitely divisible
    c. infinitely indivisible
    d. finitely indivisible

6. Match the items in Column 1 with the items in Column 2.

____ (1) fluid

____ (2) F = ma

____ (3) astrophysics

____ (4) stability

____ (5) a ball on a
flat table
top

____ (6) restoring
force in a
spring

____ (7) tides

____ (8) similar roles
to gravity
and centri-
fugal force

____ (9) viscosity

____(10) a ball sit-
ting on a
hill

a. unstable equilibrium
b. simple harmonic
motion
c. a medium which is
infinitely divisible
d. forces are in balance
and forces tend to
drive the system
toward equilibrium
e. neutral equilibrium
f. Newton's second law
of motion
g. considered long waves
h. shear force of a
fluid
i. the science of the
physical properties
and phenomena of the
stars
j. electrostatic forces
and surface tension
of the nucleus

Answers: 1. c, 2. b, 3. d, 4. d, 5. a,
6. (1) c, (2) f, (3) i, (4) d, (5) e,
(6) b, (7) g, (8) j, (9) h, (10) a

Competency 18:   Identify the general characteristics of heat.

Heat is a form of energy that may be gotten
from other forms of energy. All objects are made
of molecules that are moving. Moving molecules
have heat energy. When materials are heated, they
expand. When materials are cooled, they contract.
Heating can change solids to liquids, and liquids
to gases. Cooling can change gases to liquid and
liquids to solids. Heat depends on how fast the
molecules are moving and on how many molecules are
in the materials. Since heat is a form of energy,
any form of energy such as electrical, chemical,
and mechanical energy can be changed into heat
energy. Likewise, heat energy can be changed into
any form of energy such as electrical, chemical,
and mechanical energy. For example, when electrical energy is passed through a light bulb or the
heating element of an electric heater, the
electrical energy is changed into heat energy.
When oxygen unites with wood or coal and causes it
to burn, chemical action takes place and heat
energy is generated. Heat produced by friction
enables us to understand the nature of heat. When
two surfaces are rubbed together, friction makes
the molecules move faster, and the material becomes
hotter.

Heat is produced by change in the state of
matter. Whenever any liquid is changed into a
solid, heat is given off. Most of the heat that
is available for use comes either directly or
indirectly from the sun. A very small amount comes
from the stars. All plants and animals depend on

heat received from the sun for their existence.
We are all familiar with the heat derived from
electrical energy. (An electric light bulb gets
hot, a toaster, or electric heater.) When gases
are compressed they give off heat. When they are
allowed to expand they absorb heat. One common
result of heat is the rise in temperature of the
objects which heat is applied. Another common
result is the expansion of materials to which it
is applied. Heat will change a solid into a
liquid, and a liquid into a gas.

Heat is transferred from one place to another
in three ways: (1) Conduction, which is the process of transferring heat from molecule to molecule; (2) Convection, which is the process of
transmitting heat by means of the movement of
heated matter from one place to another; (3) and
Radiation, which is heat in the form of rays. In
both conduction and convection heat is transmitted
by moving particles. Insulation helps control
heat transference. Insulation of heat means either
to keep the heat in or keep it out of any desired
place. Units of heat measurements are the calorie
and the B. T. U. (British Thermal Unit). The
calorie is the amount of heat energy necessary to
raise the temperature of one gram of water one
degree on the centigrade scale.

Competency 19: Identify the general characteristics of light.

Light is a form of energy. Besides the
important light energy that man gets from the sun,
man can also produce light by using certain
chemicals, radioactivity, or electricity. Although
the exact nature of light is not known, there are
two theories. One theory is that light is both
wave-like and the other is that light is particu-
late. Light has a very high speed of travel
measured in round numbers about 186,000 miles per
second. Visible light is only a small part of a

larger segment of a larger spectrum called the electromagnetic spectrum. Visible light is made up of a number of components which are seen in the spectrum. The spectrum includes radio waves, infrared rays, ultraviolet rays, x-rays and gamma rays. The speed of these rays is the same in a vacuum, but they differ in wave length, frequency, and in the way which they are produced.

Bioluminescence of "cold light" is the chemical production of light by some organism. It may have different functions in different species. Light is the most important energy source to life on the earth. It is essential for green plants for it is the force that keeps the chlorophyll working. Green plants are the food for all other living things. Other organisms get the plant food directly or indirectly from green plants.

By observing the behavior of light, man has learned to make instruments, searchlights, and many other devices for studying and using light. If an object permits light to pass through it, as a clear pane of glass does, it is called trans-parent. If an object scatters the light that passes through it, as a frosted glass or a layer of milk does, it is called translucent. An object that does not permit light to pass through it is opaque. A mirror or a polished surface reflects light without scattering it. This type of reflection is called regular or specular. Some substances such as white blotting paper or freshly fallen snow reflect light in all directions. This is diffuse reflection. Light usually travels through a substance in a straight line. But it "bends" when it passes into another substance at an angle. A wedge of glass called a prism is used to bend light. This bending is called refraction. A prism breaks up white light into a spectrum because the colored light that make up the spectrum all have different wave lengths. Our eyes are sensitive to electromagnetic waves that are most abundant in sun light. The part of the spectrum of sunlight which our eyes can see is called visible radiant energy, or light. Some light also contains rays which we cannot see. Those which have shorter wave lengths that we can see are called ultra violet rays. They produce sun tan. Those that have longer wave lengths than the ones we can see are called infrared rays. These are given off by all warm objects. Actually our eyes are sensitive to only a tiny portion of all electromagnetic waves. The chief colors found in visible light are violet, blue, green, yellow, orange, and red. But by separating the colors we see more than a hundred different colors.

20

Competency 20: Identify the characteristics of sound.

Sound is a form of energy we get when objects vibrate. Slow vibrations make low sounds. Fast vibrations make high sounds. The energy of a vibrating object changes the loudness and softness of sounds. Vibrations travel as sound waves in all directions through air and other gases. Sound waves also travel through liquids and solids. Sound waves travel best and fastest through hard solids. Sound waves can be stopped by soft solids. Echoes are sound waves that bounce back. Musical instruments have vibrating strings, vibrating air columns, and vibrating solids that make sounds. Sounds can be made higher or lower by changing the length, size, tightness, and thickness of the materials that make sounds. Your voice makes sounds when air causes the vocal cords to vibrate. Lips, tongue, teeth and other parts of the mouth help you say words. The outer ear collects sound waves and sends them to the eardrum. The eardrum vibrates and passes the vibrations to other parts of the ear. Messages of sound go through the hearing nerve to the brain.

When an object vibrates, it makes the surrounding air vibrate. The vibrations are called sound waves. Sound waves travel along the back-and-forth

movement of the vibrating object that produces
them. The number of vibrations a body produces a
second is called the frequency. The speed of
sound depends upon two factors: (1) the density
of the medium through which sound waves travel,
and (2) the elasticity of the medium. The more
elastic a medium, the greater the speed of sound.
The denser a medium, the slower the speed of sound.
The speed of sound is much slower than the speed
of light.

Sound waves have different characteristics
that enable us to distinguish one kind of sound
from another. For example, musical sounds have
three distinguishing characteristics: pitch, loudness, and quality. Sounds can be classified as
either noisy or musical. A noise is produced by a
vibrating object such as a rattling window that
sends out irregular vibrations at irregular intervals. Music is made by a vibrating body that
sends out regular vibrations at regular intervals.
Some other kinds of sound include the sounds made
by people and animals, and sterophonic sound and
ultra sound. Sterophonic sound tries to reproduce
the feeling of depth, or of sounds coming from
many points, that a listener would receive if he
heard the sounds in person. Ultra sounds vibrate
frequencies too high to be heard by humans.

The unit commonly used to measure the intensity of sound is the decibel. The decibel system
is a compressed scale of measurement. The ordinary
speaking voice has an intensity of about 60
decibels. Whispering produces 10 to 20 decibels
of sounds; heavy traffic noise 70 to 80 decibels,
and thunder, 110 decibels.

Test your knowledge of competencies 18 - 20.

1. What is the name given to the type of light
    given off by organisms?
    a. reflected
    b. bioluminescence
    c. specular
    d. retracted

2. The unit used to measure the intensity for
    sound is the
    a. BTU
    b. calorie
    c. decibel
    d. kilogram

3. Three ways to transfer heat from one place to
    another are
    a. convection, conduction and radiation
    b. convection, radiation, and insulation
    c. conduction, insulation, and radiation
    d. convection, conduction, and insulation

Answers: 1. b, 2. c, 3. a

A tinkling bell starts a sound wave of condensation (air particles jammed together)
and rarefaction (air particles spread apart). The wave moves away from the bell in
all directions.

137

Competency 21: Identify the characteristics of electricty.

Electricity is a phenomenon associated with the movement of electrons during which some kind of energy removes the orbital electrons from the atoms and moves them through a conductor. The control of electricity depends on the control of the movement of electrons.

Static electricity and current electricity are two kinds of electricity. Static electricity results when matter loses electrons or pick up extra electrons. Matter with fewer electrons than protons has a positive charge of static electricity. Matter with extra electrons has a negative charge. There are two kinds of electric charges. Like electrical charges repel; unlike electric charges attract. Lightning is an abrupt discharge of electricity through the air. Lightning is a form of static electricity. Matter is essentially electrical in nature.

Electric current is the movement of electricity through a conductor and is measured in amperes. It travels through a conductor almost the speed of light.

A fuse is placed in an electric circuit to protect the circuit. It is the weakest link in the circuit.

There are two different types of electric current. Alternating current (AC) is the type we use in our home. Alternating current is produced by

generators. Direct current (DC) is the type used
in batteries. Chemicals are used in batteries to
produce electricity.

Magnetism and electricity are not the same
but they are related forms of energy. To describe
the relationship between the two, we can say that
magnetism can be used to produce electricity and
electricity can be used to produce magnetism.

Test your knowledge of competency 21.

1.   Which of the following is a false statement?
     a.   Electricity is the movement of electrons.
     b.   Matter with extra electrons has a posi-
          tive charge.
     c.   Matter with extra electrons has a nega-
          tive charge.
     d.   Like electrical charges repel.
     e.   Lightning is electricity.

2.   To produce electrical activity, we must cause
     electrons to
     a.   move
     b.   stand still
     c.   change polarity
     d.   reverse their orbits

Answers: 1. b, 2. a

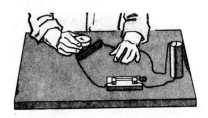

**Oersted's discovery: an electric current
flowing through a wire makes that wire behave
like a magnet.**

Competency 22:   Identify the characteristics
of magnetism.

Magnets are materials that will pick up or
attract certain things. Magnets do not attract
everything. Some metals are attracted by magnets;
others are not. Iron, steel, nickel, chromium,
and the magnetic alloys called permalloys are
attracted by magnets. Metals that are attracted
by magnets are referred to as magnetic metals.

Magnets are used in many ways. The needle in
a magnetic compass is a magnet. A magnetic compass points in a north-south direction unless it
is too near a magnetized substance. Any magnet
can be used as a compass.

The places on the magnet that are strongest
are called poles. The poles are usually located
on the ends of the magnet. The poles have more
attraction than the rest of the magnet.

A magnet's attraction is caused by a force
called magnetism. Because magnets attract magnetic
objects without touching them, magnetism must
extend beyond the magnet. Magnetism extends
farther beyond the poles of some magnets than
others. Magnetism cannot be seen. Magnetism
extends into the air around magnets. It also
extends through nonmagnetic materials that are not
too thick. Magnetism does not seem to extend
through magnetic metals.

The magnetic force of a strong magnet can be
felt when it is attracting a magnetic metal. The

magnetic force with which two strong poles attract or repel each other also can be felt. Two unlike magnetic poles attract each other and two like poles repel each other. A north and south pole attract each other. Two north or two south poles repel each other.

Small steel objects can be made into magnets by stroking them with a magnet. The magnetic material in the steel object becomes magnetized. The magnetized object has poles. A floating magnetized object acts as a magnetic compass.

A magnet can be ball-shaped. The earth is nearly spherical in shape. The earth is a huge spheroidal magnet with two magnetic poles; a north magnetic pole and a south magnetic pole. A magnet free to swing (a compass) will be attracted to another nearby magnet. The unlike poles of the two magnets will attract each other. When there is no second nearby magnet, a compass (magnet free to swing) will be moved by the magnetic poles of the magnetic earth. The swinging magnet will align itself in a north-south direction.

The magnetic poles of the earth are not in the same places as its geographic poles. Most authorities agree that the earth's north magnetic pole is located in the southern hemisphere and the earth's south magnetic pole in the northern hemisphere.

The magnetic force of a magnet extends into the area of space surrounding it. This area is called the magnet's field or magnetic field. The magnet's force in the magnetic field causes iron filings to line up in a pattern. The lines in the pattern are called the lines of force in the magnetic field. These lines of force extend from the north to the south pole of the magnet. The lines of force are concentrated at the poles. When the magnetic fields of two magnets touch, the pattern of iron filings shows that the lines of force between the magnets are attracted by unlike poles or repelled by like poles.

A magnetic field surrounds a wire when it is carrying a current of electricity. One way the magnetic field around a wire carrying a current of electricity can be strengthened is by coiling the wire into a smaller area.

An iron core is temporarily magnetized if it is inserted in the magnetic field that surrounds a coil of wire carrying a current of electricity. Steel is permanently magnetized if it is inserted in the magnetic field that surrounds a coil of wire carrying an electric current.

An electromagnet is a magnet whose magnetism can be "turned on and off." It is made by coiling insulated copper wire around an iron core. The core is temporarily magnetized by the magnetic field surrounding the coil of wire in which an electric current is flowing. It is a temporary magnet because the core is a magnet only when the current is flowing through the coil wire. An electromagnet can be made stronger by winding more turns of wire around the core, by increasing the size of the core, and by increasing the amount of current. The three methods can be used at the same time to increase the strength of an electromagnet. The electromagnet is "turned off" by stopping the flow of electricity.

The fact that an electromagnet is a temporary magnet is the essential principle underlying the functioning of the telegraph, the electric motor, the telephone and many other devices. A motor has two magnets. The outside magnet is an electromagnet. Inside of this magnet there is another magnet. The inside magnet spins around when electricity flows through the electromagnet. When the inside magnet spins, it makes whatever is hooked up to it move. Electromagnets are used in many of the things in the home, such as an electric doorbell, blender, and in many electric toys.

A lodestone is a natural magnet. It was magnetized by the earth's magnetic field of force.

A magnet seems to be made of little magnets
whose north poles lines up in one direction and
south poles in an opposite direction. These little magnets may be the atoms of magnetic metal of
which the magnet is made. The magnetism of a
substance is due essentially to the magnetic properties of its atoms and to the arrangement of its
atoms. The magnetic behavior of an atom depends
on the spin of its electrons. Not all the
answers regarding the cause of the force called
magnetism are known.

Summary

The space around a magnet can act like a magnet. This space, around which the force of a magnet acts or is felt, is called the magnetic field.
The earth is a magnetic field where magnetism can
be found. Magnetic fields lie around every magnet.

The properties of a magnetic field can be
demonstrated by sprinkling iron filings around a
magnet. The filings will arrange themselves into
a pattern of lines. These lines are called lines
of force. There will be more lines of force at
the ends (poles) of the magnet, where the magnetic
force is strongest, than at the middle of the magnet. There are fewer lines farther away from the
poles, showing that the field becomes weaker in
those areas.

Test your knowledge of competency 22.

1. A magnetic field is the area
    a. around the ends of a magnet
    b. along the sides of a magnet
    c. around the magnet
    d. under the magnet.

2. The magnetic field is strongest
   a. at the poles where the lines of force are farther apart
   b. at the poles where the lines of force are closer together
   c. at the center where the lines of force are concentrated
   d. at the center where the lines of force are fewer

3. A magnetic field may be defined as the
   a. area occupied by the lines of force radiating from a charged object
   b. area between the poles of the magnet
   c. area through which electronic movement occurs within an insulator
   d. area around a magnet which can affect another magnetic material

Answers: 1. c, 2. b, 3. d

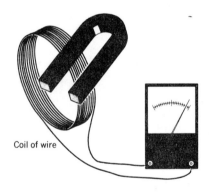

Coil of wire

Faraday's discovery: a magnet moved near a coil of wire causes an electric current to flow in the wire.

Competency 23-1: Describe the solar system and identify some relationships among its components.

Space

What with plants and moons in orbit up there,
And constellations and comets most everywhere,
And nebulas floating among the stars,
And strange looking objects called quasars,
And meteors and galaxies in every place,
Where, in all the heavens, is there space?

Helen Jeffries

The members of our solar system are heavenly bodies called satellites which revolve around the sun. The large nine bodies, or planets, are the main components. These include Mercury, Venus, Earth, Mars, Jupiter, Saturn, Uranus, Neptune, and Pluto. The other components include asteroids, that circle the sun between Mars and Jupiter, comets, meteors, and meteorites.

At the center of our solar system is a huge star which is the sun. The sun gives off light from nuclear reactions while planets reflect this light from the sun or other stars. The sun makes life on earth possible. Our sun is one of 100 billion stars in our Milky Way galaxy.

Everything in the universe is in motion. The planets travel in orbits around the sun which are oval in shape and all planets revolve in a counter-clockwise direction. The planets spin or rotate

145

on an axis. One rotation is the planet's day
while one revolution around the sun is a year.
Thirty-five satellites of the planets have been
discovered which are called moons. Jupiter has
the greatest number with fourteen moons. Planets
revolve around the sun as a result of two conditions: inertia and gravity. Inertia causes a
body that is moving to remain in motion. Gravitational pull from the sun causes the planets to
stay in their orbits.

Mercury is the nearest planet to the sun as
well as the smallest. It has neither air nor
water and has extremely hot temperatures. Venus
is about the size of Earth and is surrounded by
thick clouds which trap the sun's heat. It is
believed the clouds contain ten percent carbon
dioxide and some water vapor.

The Earth revolves around the sun once every
365¼ days. It is tilted on its axis which results
in the different seasons of the year. Changes in
weather occur because of moving air masses, air
pressure differences, and changes in water vapor,
all caused by the sun. The earth has one moon
with no atmosphere or water. Only one side is
viewed from the earth because of the moon's rotation on its axis. Its phases are the results of
its revolution around the earth. The earth's
gravitational pull keeps the moon in orbit and the
moon's pull affects the earth in the form of tides.

Mars is next to earth and moves closer to
earth every 15 years. It has two small moons.
Mars is like the earth in that they both have seasons. It has ice caps at its poles and the surface also changes color with the seasons. Mars is
believed to have deserts and an atmosphere thinner
than the earth's. It has extreme temperature
changes between day and night.

Between Mars and Jupiter are asteroids also
called planetoids. They look like stars but are
really little planets which revolve around the sun.

They consist of irregular lumps of rock and metal.

Jupiter, the largest planet, has 14 moons. This planet does not show a solid surface but does show shifting belts of clouds in colored bands. It is believed to be a solid core of rock and metal. Jupiter is known for its red spot and has an atmosphere of thick gases.

Saturn has ten moons and is surrounded by seven broad but thin rings revolving around its equator. These are believed to be pieces of rock or grains of sand. Uranus, with five moons, has eight rings around it. Unlike Saturn, the rings are narrow and faint. It rotates on almost a horizontal axis while other planets are on a vertical axis. Uranus and Neptune are called the "twin planets" because they both have a solid core and are surrounded by an icy layer as well as an atmosphere of the same kinds of gases. They are both about the same size. Neptune has two moons. Pluto, the farthest from the sun, has one moon. It revolves around the sun once in about 248 years.

Comets have long, oval-shaped orbits that bring them close to the sun and then far out again. It does not have a tail until it nears the sun. The tail is very thin streams of melted gases and when the comet travels away from the sun, they freeze and disappear. The comet's head consists of small rocks, dust, and frozen gases; these melt and change to vapor as they near the sun. A comet also reflects the sun's light. The most famous one, Halley's commet, returns every 76 years. Some never return if they're destroyed near a larger body.

The last components of the solar system are meteors and meteorites. These are rocks in space made of tiny grains of sand or may contain iron and nickel, or silicates. When the earth passes these rocks, friction occurs causing them to burn and make a bright streak, sometimes referred to as "shooting stars." If a meteor makes it to the earth's surface before it burns up, it is called a meteorite. Craters in Arizona and Canada were probably formed by meteorites.

Our solar system is not unique. It is believed there are other galaxies that resemble our own. The origin of our solar system is explained by many theories. The most popular one is the dust cloud theory in which the solar system was formed by huge clouds of gases and dusts. Our sun was believed to have been formed by a nuclear reaction. This theory also explains the formation of all the stars and their satellites.

Test your knowledge of competency 23-1.

1. Which planet is most like the Earth?
    a. Jupiter
    b. Mars
    c. Mercury
    d. Neptune
    e. Comet

2. Which component of the solar system has a tail as it nears the sun?
    a. nebulas
    b. meteors
    c. quasars
    d. comets
    e. satellites

Answers: 1. b, 2. d

Competency 23-2: Describe the solar system and identify some relationships among its components.

The word "solar" comes from the Latin word sol, which means "sun." The sun and all the traveling bodies around it make up the solar system. These heavenly bodies are called satellites. A satellite is any heavenly body that travels around another heavenly body.

The major members of the solar system are nine large bodies called planets. The word "planet" means "wanderer." The planets were given this name because they do seem to wander over the sky instead of staying in one position as a star. The names of the planets in order by distance from the sun are: Mercury, Venus, Earth, Mars, Jupiter, Saturn, Uranus, Neptune, and Pluto.

Planets are not stars because stars shine and give off light. Planets, however, shine because they reflect the light of the sun or of other stars. In size, planets are much smaller than the sun and most of the stars.

The planets travel in elliptical or oval paths called an orbit around the sun. The planets move or revolve in a counterclockwise direction from west to east around the sun. One complete revolution is called the planet's year. As the planets revolve around the sun, they rotate around an imaginary line, called an axis, which runs through the north and south poles of the planet. One complete rotation of the planet on its axis is called the planet's day.

Many of the planets have their own small satellites that revolve around them. We call these satellites moons. There have been thirty-five moons discovered in our solar system: one for Earth, two for Mars, fourteen for Jupiter, ten for Saturn, five for Uranus, two for Neptune, and one for Pluto.

The planets of our solar system are alike in many ways and yet differ in just as many ways. They all are satellites of the sun and they re-volve around the sun while rotating on their axis. They obtain their energy from the sun. They all contain the same basic chemicals, although the proportions are different.

The nine planets of our solar system differ in their distance from the sun and in their size

and weight. Also, each planet has a different
kind and amount of atmosphere. The length of time
it takes for a complete revolution of a planet and
its rotation is also different. The planets
differ in the number of moons they have, as well.

Besides the nine planets in our solar system
there are at least 1,500 little planets called
asteroids. Also, there are hundreds of comets, the
very strange heavenly bodies that have tails
streaming out from them. There are, too, great
swarms of meteors. Meteors are pieces of metal or
rock, sometimes no bigger than grains of sand.
Many meteors are pulled to the planets. They become white hot when they fall and are given the
names shooting stars or fireballs.

There is only one true star in the solar
system, the sun itself. All the other stars are
far beyond the outermost planet.

****

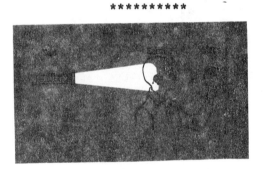

A DEMONSTRATION OF AN ECLIPSE OF THE MOON

**The teacher must help in translating what
is seen in the demonstration and what actually
happens in the sky.**

THE PLANETS
Drawn to scale in this diagram but not the
distances between their orbits

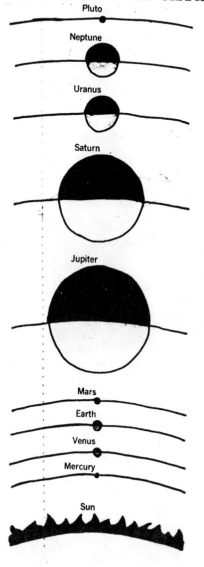

To remember use this
code.

Mr. VEM J. SUNP

Mercury
Venus
Earth
Mars
Jupiter

Saturn
Uranus
Neptune
Pluto

Test your knowledge of competency 23-2.

1. What is the only true star in our solar
   system?
   a. Saturn
   b. the sun
   c. meteor
   d. Mars

2. How many planets make up the major components
   of our solar system?
   a. six
   b. ten
   c. nine
   d. twelve

Answers: 1. b, 2. c

****

A DEMONSTRATION OF AN ECLIPSE OF THE SUN

The teacher must help in translating what
is seen in the demonstration and what actually
happens in the sky.

Competency 24:   Identify the relationship of
the earth's size and shape to its rotation and
revolution.

The earth is almost completely round. At the
equator, the distance around the earth is 24,902
miles. At the poles, the earth measures 24,860
miles around. The distance through the earth at
the equator is 7,927 miles. The distance through
the earth at the poles is about 7,900 miles.

The difference in distance through and around
the earth at the equator and at the poles is
caused by the centrifugal force produced by the
rotation of the Earth. Rotation is the turning
motion of a body on its axis. As the earth rotates, or turns on its axis, it bulges out at the
equator and tends to remain flat at the poles.

The moving of a planet about the sun is revolution. Each planet revolves around the sun at
different rates. The relationship can be explained by Newton's Law of Gravitation. He said
that all objects attract each other, and that the
force of their attraction depends upon the sizes
of the objects and the distance between them. The
force of attraction is in direct proportion to the
product of their masses. This means, the larger
the mass of the planet, the greater the attraction.
The force is also in inverse proportion to the
square of the distance between the planets and the
sun. This means, the farther apart the planet is
from the sun, the less the gravitation. Therefore,
as the Earth makes a revolution or revolves around
the sun, the orbit is determined by the mass of the
Earth and its distance from the sun.

GRAVITY AND INERTIA TOGETHER ACT ON A PLANET IN SUCH A WAY THAT THE PLANET REVOLVES AROUND THE SUN

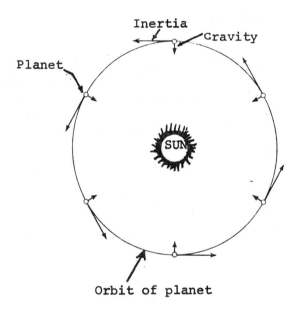

Test your knowledge of competency 24.

1. The force that causes the earth to bulge out at the equator is
   a. rotation
   b. revolution
   c. centrifugal force
   d. gravity

2. The turning of a body on its axis is
   a. rotation
   b. revolution
   c. centripetal force
   d. centrifugal force

3. The relationship between the earth's size and shape to revolution can be explained by
   a. rotation
   b. revolution
   c. centrifugal force
   d. Newton's Law of Gravitation

Answers: 1. c, 2. a, 3. d

Competency 25: Define the role of space travel as it relates to advancements in the area of communication.

Space exploration has done a lot of things for the world in which we live, but the greatest area of advancement has been in communications. In 1946 Arthur C. Clark suggested the global concept of a communications system consisting of three satellites placed at certain altitudes. In 1955 John R. Pierce analyzed two methods for communicating via satellites. One method was to reflect signals off a passive satellite that would have no electronic equipment. The second method was to transmit to an active satellite that would have equipment for receiving and amplifying the signal and transmitting them to earth.

The first voice transmission from a satellite occurred on December 19, 1958, when President Eisenhower's Christmas message was carried to the world by an orbiting Atlas missil with simple signal repetition equipment aboard. This event provided a unique initial demonstration of the promise of communications satellites.

On July 10, 1962, Telstar I, designed by the Bell System, relayed the first transmission of television signals between the United States and Europe; six days later, it relayed color television signals. Telstar I traveled at a low altitude and did not provide continuous service.

Early Bird, the first commercial communications satellite was placed in orbit over the Atlantic

156

Ocean on April 6, 1956. This satellite provided one television channel or 240 two-way telephone circuits. Early Bird later went into retirement over the Atlantic.

Three satellites of the Intelsat II series were launched during 1967. These satellites had the same television-channel and telephone-circuit capacity as Early Bird, but they extended satellite coverage to two-thirds of the world.

Three satellites of the Intelsat III series were launched in 1968 and 1969. This established the first global communications system. This system was envisioned by the United States in 1962, when Congress passed the Communications Satellite Act, and by the International Telecommunications Satellite Consortium which was formed in 1964 to establish a global system as a joint international venture. Each satellite in this series provided 1,200 telephone circuits or four television channels.

Giant satellites of the Intelsat IV series were launched in 1971. Each satellite provided twelve television channels and 9,000 telephone circuits.

In 1977 several domestic communication satellites were launched, which, for the first time, linked ships at sea with world-wide telecommunications networks. The Communication Technology Satellite, a joint United States-Canadian venture, was also launched. The CTS was to test the concept of broadcasting from space to individual rooftops.

In 1973 there were 50 earth stations in nearly 35 countries. These earth stations transmit and receive communications traffic.

International Communication via satellite require multilateral agreements. At least 73 countries signed two international agreements in

157

Washington, D.C., in 1964. These agreements call for financial support of the satellite system and provide a seat on the governing body of the International Telecommunication Satellite Consortium.

The Soviet Union has also been involved in communication via satellite. The Soviet Union launched its first communication satellite, Molniya I, on April 23, 1965. Since then a series of Molniya satellites has been launched as part of the USSR's "orbita" communications network. The Molniya satellites are used for a variety of domestic communications, such as T.V. distribution between some 30 earth stations extending from Moscow to Vladivostok.

Many advances have been made in communication because of our space explorations. Many new advances are expected in the coming years.

Test your knowledge of competency 25.

1. The first thoughts of communication via satellite were voiced in?
   a. 1936
   b. 1946
   c. 1963
   d. 1955

2. Which of the following satellites has not electronic equipment on board?
   a. Active satellite
   b. Passive satellite
   c. Early Bird
   d. Echo I

3. Which of the following are false?
   a. The U.S. is far ahead of the USSR in the area of communications.
   b. Arthus C. Clark analyzed two methods of communicating via satellite.
   c. The first transmission via satellite was in 1968.
   d. All of the above are false.

Answers: 1. b, 2. b, 3. d

Competency 26:   Identify the characteristics
of moisture as related to humidity, the water
cycle, clouds, and precipitation.

Water enters the air through a process called
evaporation. Evaporation takes place when water
changes from a liquid to a gas called water vapor.
Evaporation takes place because the molecules in
water are moving. The faster moving molecules,
near the surface of the water, leave and go off
into the air as water vapor.

There are several factors that effect the
speed of evaporation. These are:

1.   Heat. Heat will cause water molecules to
move faster, this will in turn speed up the process of evaporation.

2.   The size of a body of water. A large
body of water will experience faster evaporation
as more molecules can leave the water at the same
time.

3.   The amount of water already in the air.
If there is a great deal of water already in the
air evaporation will be slow.

4.   Winds. Winds blow away air that is
filled with water vapor. This speeds the process
of evaporation.

5.   Air pressure. Low air pressure means the
air is not pressing as hard on the surface of the
water. This allows the water vapor to leave the

159

surface of the water and enter the atmosphere.

When water vapor changes into a liquid the change is called condensation. When air containing water vapor is cooled the molecules move more slowly and some closer together. If the air is cooled enough the water vapor molecules come close enough together to form water again. The temperature below which the air must be cooled for condensation is called the dew point.

When a large layer of air next to the earth's surface is cooled below its dew point a fog is formed. The water droplets in a fog are heavier than the air but they are so small and fall so slowly that the smallest air movement will keep them floating.

Clouds are formed when a mass of air is cooled. When warm air containing water vapor rises in the air it becomes colder. The warm rising air eventually reaches levels where the air pressure is less and the air expands. When the air expands it uses some of its energy and becomes colder. If the air is cooled below its dew point a cloud is formed. The water droplets in a cloud are heavier than air but they are so small and fall so slowly that the slightest air movement will keep them afloat.

The shapes of clouds are determined by the way they are formed. If the movement of the cooling air is verticle the clouds form huge billowy masses. If the movement of the cooling air is horizontal the clouds form layers.

When moisture falls from the air it is called precipitation. The forms of precipitation are:

1. Rain. Rain is the water that falls from a cloud. When enough water droplets are joined they become too heavy to be supported by the wind and must fall to earth.

2. Drizzle. Drizzle is made up of very fine cloud droplets. Drizzle falls to earth when there is no wind to support the clouds.

3. Snow. Snow forms from water vapor that condenses when the temperature of the air is below freezing. The water vapor condenses into ice crystals or snow.

4. Sleet. Sleet is frozen rain. It is usually formed during the winter when raindrops fall through a below-freezing layer of air near the ground.

5. Hail. Hail is usually formed during summer thunderstorms. When there are strong upward currents of air in a thundercloud raindrops fall towards the earth but are swept up to below-freezing temperatures and turn to ice. As they begin to fall again they are coated with another layer of water and are once again swept up to freezing temperatures. This cycle continues until the hailstone is too heavy to be swept upwards.

All the water on the earth is constantly evaporating to form water vapor. This water vapor is constantly condensing back into water. This never ending cycle of evaporation and condensation is called the hydrologic or water cycle.

Test your knowledge of competency 26.

1. Water enters the air through a process called
    a. osmosis
    b. evaporation
    c. condensation
    d. precipitation

2. The temperature below which air must be cooled for condensation is called the
    a. dew point
    b. hydrologic cycle
    c. frost line
    d. condensation point

Answers: 1. b, 2. a

Competency 27-1: Describe the characteristics of air masses and fronts that cause storms.

Air masses are huge bodies of air that may cover a vast portion of the earth's surface and may be very wide and quite wide.

Air masses are named according to the part of the earth's surface in which they are formed.

1. Those formed in the tropics are called tropical, and are warm.

2. Those that are formed in the polar regions are called polar and are cold.

3. Air masses from continents are continental and are dry.

4. Air masses from oceans are called maritime and are moist or humid.

As a result, there are 4 possible kinds of air masses.

1. Continental tropical air masses are dry and warm.

2. The maritime tropical air mass is moist and warm.

3. Continental polar air masses are dry and cold.

4. The maritime polar air mass is moist and

162

cold.

The air masses that affect the weather in North America come from six different areas.

1. Polar Canadian air masses are formed over north-central Canada, move southeasterly, and are cold and dry. They bring cold waves in winter and in summer they bring cool, dry weather.

2. Polar Atlantic air masses are formed over the northern Atlantic Ocean. They move easterly, are cold and moist. In winter they bring cold, cloudy weather and some light precipitation. In the summer they bring cool weather with clouds and fogs.

3. Polar Pacific air masses are formed over the northern Pacific Ocean. They travel southward, they are cool rather than cold, and are very moist. In the winter they bring rain and snow, and in summer they bring cool, foggy weather.

4. Tropical Continental air masses are formed over Mexico and southwest U.S. They usually move northeasterly over central U.S. They are warm and dry and affect North America only in the summer when they bring dry, clean, and very hot weather.

5. Tropical Atlantic air masses are formed over the tropical part of the Atlantic Ocean and the Gulf of Mexico. They move northeasterly, are warm and moist. In winter they bring mild weather, and in summer they bring hot, humid weather and thunderstorms.

6. Tropical Pacific air masses are formed in the tropical part of the Pacific Ocean. They move northeasterly, and are warm and moist. They affect the Pacific coast only in winter and they bring cool, foggy weather.

Weather Fronts

A front is when two air masses meet. There are two kinds of fronts.

1. A warm front is caused by warm air pushing colder air ahead of it. When a warm front advances, warm air moves up over the retreating cold air. When the warm air rises, it becomes cool, and the water vapor in the air condenses to form large masses of clouds along the entire front. The rains produced by a warm front cover a wide area, are usually steady, and last until the warm front passes.

2. A cold front is when cold air is pushing warmer air ahead of it. When a cold front advances, the cold air pushes under the warm air that is retreating, and lifts up this warm air. As the warm air is lifted up quickly, it cools, and the water vapor condenses. The rains produced by a cold front cover a smaller area, are violent, and last only a short time.

A stationary front is the boundary line between a cold air mass and a warm air mass when both air masses stop and do not move for several days. The weather produced by a stationary front is about the same as that produced by a warm front.

Sometimes an occluded front is formed when a warm air mass is lifed up by the cold air mass behind it. There is no change in temperature of the air because there is only a change from one mass of cold air to another.

Test your knowledge of competency 27-1.

1. The air masses formed in the polar regions
    are called
    a. Continental
    b. Tropical
    c. Polar
    d. Maritime
    e. cold front

2. The boundary line between a cold air mass and
    a warm air mass is a
    a. warm front
    b. cold front
    c. occluded front
    d. stationary front

3. A _____ is when 2 air masses meet.
    a. front
    b. air masses
    c. tropical
    d. ocean

Answers: 1. c, 2. d, 3. a

Competency 27-2: Describe the characteristics
of air masses and fronts that cause storms.

When a body of air takes on physical characteristics which distinguish it from the other air
surrounding the earth, it is referred to as an air
mass. The main distinguishing characteristics are
temperature and moisture content. Air masses differ greatly from each other, and the weather that
an air mass will bring depends mostly on the
particular temperature and humidity that it has.
An air mass is formed when the atmosphere stays
quietly over a certain part of the earth's surface
until it picks up the temperature and humidity of
that part of the earth's surface.

Air masses are classified according to the
surface and general latitude of their source

regions:

Surface	Latitude
Maritime (m)	Artic (A)
Continental (c)	Polar (P)
	Tropical (T)
	Equatorial (E)

As a result, there are four possible kinds of air masses.

1. The continental tropical (cT) air mass is dry and warm.

2. The maritime tropical (mT) air mass is moist and warm.

3. The continental polar (cP) air mass is cold and dry.

4. The maritime polar (mP) air mass is cold and moist.

Once an air mass is formed, it is influenced to a great extent by the earth's general circulation patterns and it is carried to another place by the general movements of the atmosphere.

The air masses that affect the weather in North America come from six different areas.

1. Polar Canadian (cP) air masses are formed over north-central Canada.

2. Polar Atlantic (mP) air masses are formed over the northern Atlantic Ocean.

3. Polar Pacific (mP) air masses are formed over the northern Pacific Ocean.

4. Tropical Atlantic (mT) air masses are formed over the tropical part of the Atlantic Ocean and the Gulf of Mexico.

5. Tropical Continental (cT) air masses are formed over Mexico and southwest United States.

6. Tropical Pacific (mT) air masses are formed over the tropical part of the Pacific Ocean.

The boundary between two air masses is called a front. There are two common kinds of fronts. A warm front is the boundary of an advancing warm air mass over a colder surface and a cold front is the boundary of a cold air mass moving over a warmer surface. These boundaries may vary in width from a few miles to a wide frontal zone of over 100 miles. It is along these fronts, which divide air masses of different physical characteristics, that drastic changes of weather occur.

A stationary front is the boundary line between a cold air mass and a warm air mass when both air masses stop and do not move for several days. Sometimes an occluded front is formed when a warm air mass, which lies between two cold air masses, is lifted up by the cold air mass behind it.

The air masses that move across earth differ in air pressure. Cold air masses have higher pressures than warm air masses. This difference occurs because cold air is heavier than warm air, and it can exert more pressure than warm air.

An area of low pressure is called a low, or a cyclone. The lowest air pressure in a low is at its center. Wave cyclones are formed by air moving in opposite directions along a front. As the cyclonic wave fully develops, a low-pressure area of storm center spins off. The low moves away, carrying with it rising air currents, clouds, precipitation, and generally bad weather. Low, or cyclones, are therefore, generally associated with poor weather.

Highs, or anticyclones, on the other hand are generally associated with good weather. The

167

highest air pressure in a high is at its center. As a result, air blows outward from the center of the high.

The lows in the United States start in the northwest, southwest and southeast. Highs in the United States can start either in polar or tropical regions.

Hurricanes are lows, or cyclones, that form in the tropics over the ocean where the sun heats huge masses of moist air and an ascending spiral motion results. The hurricane gains energy from its source region and although the winds in a hurricane blow at a great speed, the hurricane itself moves rather slowly. The biggest damage produced by a hurricane is caused by the waves it produces. (These lows or cyclones have different names in different parts of the earth.)

1. West Indies - Hurricanes

2. Western Pacific Ocean - typhoons

3. Indian Ocean - Cyclones

4. Australia - Willy-willies

5. Philippine Island - banguios

The breeding grounds of the hurricanes which mostly affect the United States are in the Atlantic Ocean southeast of the Caribbean Sea.

Tornadoes are the smallest, most violent, and most short-lived of all storms. Although it may have less total energy than other storms, the concentration of its energy in a relatively small region gives this storm its violent distinction. Characterized by a whirling, funnel-shaped cloud that hangs from a dark cloud mass, the tornado is commonly referred to as a twister.

Tornadoes occur around the world, but are

most prevalent in the United States and Australia. The complete mechanism of tornado formation is not known, due to its many variables. One essential component is rising air which occurs in thunderstorm formation and in the meeting of cold and warm air masses. This condition is frequently fulfilled during the spring and summer in the midwestern United States where tornadoes are common.

A great deal of tornado damage results from the sudden' reduction in air pressure as it passes and the violent winds. Wind, rain, and thunderstorms usually precede a tornado as the result of the frontal activity associated with its formation. The wind damage accompanying a tornado is enormous. The center is also very destructive because the air pressure within the funnel is very low.

A tornado occurring over water is known as a waterspout. The waterspout has very little water in it. Most of the bottom part is a fine spray with perhaps a few feet of water at the bottom.

Storms are atmospheric disturbances associated with vertical air motion that may develop locally within a single air mass or due to frontal activity between two air masses. There are various types of storms.

The thunderstorm is a rainstorm distinguished by thunder and lightning and sometimes hail. Thunderstorms may result from frontal cyclonic disturbances or strong local heating. A thunderstorm is short, rarely lasting more than two hours, but it is possible to have many thunderstorms in a day.

The lightning of a thunderstorm is a discharge of electrical energy. Lightning can flow between the bottom and top of the same cloud, between two clouds of different charges, from a cloud to the earth, and sometimes even from the earth to a cloud. Lightning is seen first and then the thunder is heard next.

The sudden release of energy of a lightning stroke explosively heats the air producing the compression we hear as thunder. The sound compressions travel out from different parts of the lightning stroke. Rumbling thunder is partially due to the varying distances between the observer and the different portions of the lightning stroke. The rumbling of thunder is also a series of echoes produced when thunder is reflected many times by the clouds.

When a warm air mass overrides a cold air mass, rain may form. The rain falls to earth through the underlying cold air. If the temperature of the earth's surface is below 32°F and the raindrops do not freeze before striking the earth, the rain will freeze on the cold objects on which it falls. A large layer of ice builds up on the objects exposed to the freezing rain. The resultant glaze is referred to as an ice storm.

Snow is made up of ice crystals that fall from ice clouds. A snowstorm is an appreciable accumulation of snow. When a snowstorm is accompanied by high winds and low temperatures, the storm is referred to as a blizzard. The winds whip the fallen snow into blending swirls. Visibility may be reduced to a few inches. For this reason, a blizzard is often called a blinding snowstorm.

Test your knowledge of competency 27-2.

1. The biggest damage produced by a hurricane is caused by the _____ it produces.
   a. winds
   b. waves
   c. heat
   d. rain

2. Tornadoes occur around the world, but are most prevalent in the _____.
   a. tropical regions
   b. Polar Pacific area
   c. Polar Atlantic area
   d. United States and Australia

3. A/an _____ is the boundary line between a cold air mass and a warm air mass when both air masses stop and do not move for several days.
   a. stationary front
   b. cold front
   c. occluded front
   d. warm front

Answers: 1. b, 2. d, 3. a

Competency 28:   Identify the information
necessary for accurate weather forecasting.

Weather includes all the changes in temperature, wind, air pressure, and moisture. Weather
plays an important part in our daily lives. We
make our plans according to weather forecasts.

Observations are made at weather stations
throughout the world. Accurate forecasting depends on these observations. The information is
analyzed and forecasters base their predictions on
the patterns that highs, lows, and other weather
elements usually follow. Since weather systems do
not always act in the same way and no two weather
systems are exactly alike, it is difficult to make
accurate long range predictions. Short term forecasts tend to be much more accurate.

Weather forecasts can be made only if the
forecaster knows present and past conditions of
large areas. Weather conditions are recorded at
weather stations throughout the world. Air pressure, temperature, humidity, wind speed and directions, cloud forms, amounts of rain and snow, and
such obstructions to visibility as fog, haze, and
smoke are reported. Weather is also reported by
airplane pilots, radar operators, and crew members
on ships at sea. The information is condensed and
transmitted by radio and teletype to the United
States National Weather Service.

The weatherman is really a specially trained
scientist in meteorology (the science of the atmosphere). So a more accurate name for a

weatherman is meteorologist. Meteorologists assemble the weather reports received from all over the world. They study radar pictures and data received from weather satellites, and carefully determine what kind of weather is moving toward us.

Meteorologists use many instruments in their work which indicate temperature, air pressure, wind speed and direction, rainfall, humidity, the kinds of clouds in the sky, and other important information. Some of the instruments used for making these measurements are the thermometer, barometer, wind vane, anemometer, rain gauge, and hygrometer. Notice that some of these end in "meter" a Greek word meaning "measure."

The meteorologist wants to know about the air near him. But he also wants the same information about the upper air.

Large helium-filled balloons are sent up to obtain data about the air fifteen or more miles above the ground. A radiosonde is attached to the baloon. This instrument transmits the data to receivers on the ground. Afterward the radiosonds parachutes back to earth and is recovered.

The future of weather forecasting is bright. Weather satellites in space continuously survey weather patterns over the entire earth and transmit data to the ground where computers process it and meteorologists interpret it. Airplanes and satellites are used to track severe storms such as hurricanes. This makes possible earlier warnings to air and sea craft, and to land areas that will be affected. The capabilities of these satellites are being developed and improved constantly to make longer term weather predictions more accurate.

Test your knowledge of competency 28.

1. A scientist who is specially trained to study
    the atmosphere is a
    a. paleontologist
    b. radiologist
    c. meteorologist

2. Which of the following instruments are not
    used in making measurements for predicting
    weather?
    a. radiosonde
    b. thermometer
    c. hydrometer
    d. hygrometer
    e. none of the above

3. Weather includes all the changes in
    a. temperature
    b. wind
    c. air pressure
    d. moisture
    e. a, b, c, and d

Answers: 1. c, 2. c, 3. e

Competency 29: Identify the components of climate and its effect on natural (native) flora and fauna.

Climate is the average weather of a place over a period of years. The factors of climate can be divided into two classes. The first class consists of those factors that control the yearly temperature of a particular place, and the second class consists of those factors that control the yearly rainfall of that place. The factors that control temperature are discussed first.

Latitude, or distance from the equator, influences temperature more than any other factor. The higher the latitude of a place, the colder its climate will be. Altitude is the height above sea level, and the higher the altitude of a place, the colder its climate will be. Land and water masses affect the climate of a place, because land masses heat up and cool down more quickly than water masses. The direction of the prevailing winds affects the climate of a continent's seacoast. Mountain ranges and plains determine how much faraway winds affect a region's climate. Ocean currents can make the climate of a region much warmer or colder than normal for the region's latitude.

There are also six factors that control the yearly rainfall. Latitude affects the amount of rainfall a region receives, because it determines in which wind belt a region will be located during the year. These windbelts shift during the year as the earth revolves around the sun, so some

175

places may be in a rainy belt for part of the year and in a dry belt for another part of the year. Sometimes seasonal wind changes give a region a dry season and a wet season. Mountains affect the amount of rainfall a region will receive. Windward sides of the mountains receive more rainfall than the leeward sides. Winds from the ocean give regions nearest the ocean the most rainfall. The warmer the ocean the heavier the rainfall will be. Ocean currents affect rainfall as well as temperature. When ocean currents are much warmer or colder than the land or water around them, much fog is formed.

The effect of climate on native flora and fauna varies as the climate varies. Considering the hot, wet climate at or near the equator, we find a heavy growth of plants forming a jungle. Animals may be very large because of an abundance of food and have short hair to keep cool. Reptiles and insects are teeming since there is a plentiful water supply and a favorable egg-laying environment.

Moving farther from the equator, it is still hot with varying wet and dry seasons. Mostly coarse grasses, spring plants, and a few trees grow in these regions. Animal life is not so plentiful as in the tropical rainforest, but some of the same creatures may be found there in the rainy season. As the dry season approaches, these animals migrate toward water or die.

The desert climate, farther from the equator is extremely hot and dry. The few plants there have smaller leaves with their chlorophyll nearer the surface. The stems are upright to facilitate water storage. The root system penetrates a very large area, and many plants grow spines for protection agains thirsty animals. Blossoms grow quickly and seeds are specialized so as to sprout only when soaked with water. This is to prevent sprouting after a brief shower only to dry up and die.

Animals are usually small in hot, dry areas. They need little water. The kangaroo rat, for instance, drinks no water even in captivity. It produces its own water supply from its high carbohydrate diet. It has no sweat glands and has very efficient kidneys. Birds are also well adapted to this climate as their own body temperature may go as high as 108°F. They fly fast, taking advantage of the cooling effect of circulating air.

Lack of water is also a problem in the high mountain climate, because the moisture is frozen. Plants tend to have slender needlelike leaves instead of broad surfaces which evaporate moisture and wilt. They are low-growing and often grow in protection of a large rock. Animals are few because of these adverse conditions. They are frequently furry or wooly and eat other animals as well as plants.

In the intensely cold climates, there is almost no plant or animal life except water creatures. One animal, the emperor penguin, spends a great deal of its time on the edges of ice floes feeding on fish and small shrimplike animals. Strangely enough, insects are found there because their built-in antifreeze permits them to survive the winter completely inactive and revive again in the spring. Other animals, especially birds, simply migrate to warmer areas during the winter. Many others, as cold weather approaches, grow thicker coats to keep them warm.

An unusual tree, the arctic willow, shows an interesting adaptation to the cold. Instead of growing upright like a normal tree, it grows in matlike form close to the ground. Its leaves are small and fuzzy to prevent loss of moisture when the strong winds sweep across the tundra.

Test your knowledge of competency 29.

1. Climate is the
    a. altitude of an area
    b. average temperature over many years
    c. average weather of a place over a period
        of years
    d. condition of the atmosphere at a particu-
        lar time and place

2. Which is a factor of the yearly rainfall of
    an area?
    a. latitude and longitude
    b. ocean currents and tidal waves
    c. land and water masses and altitude
    d. wind belts and ocean currents

3. Which describes a plant in a hot, dry climate?
    a. broad, green leaves
    b. wide, thin leaves
    c. thorny, fleshy leaves
    d. low, creeping flowers

Answers: 1. c, 2. d, 3. c

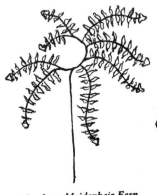

Northern Maidenhair Fern
(Adiantum pedatum)

Staghorn Fern
(Platycerium bifurcatum)

178

Competency 30: Identify the physical characteristics of the earth's structure.

In order to identify the composition and features of the earth's surface, a brief explanation of how the earth was formed must be made.

The earth was a huge ball of hot gases. As it began to cool, it started to contract. Most of the material changed from a gas into a liquid. The heavier materials settled toward the center and the lighter materials floated to the top where it formed molten rock. The rest of the materials remained as hot gases above the surface of the liquid. As it continued to cool, a solid crust was formed on top of the liquid. As the crust contracted and broke open, more molten rock flowed out through these openings. It cooled and formed solid rock. Over a long period of time bodies of water were eventually formed through water vapor and rain.

The earth is made up of three separate layers: the crust, the mantle, and the core. The crust is a very thin outer layer of rock. The raised parts of the rock form the earth's continents and the lower parts form the ocean floors. The crust is thickest under the continents and thinnest under the oceans.

The tremendous forces inside the earth are constantly acting on the crust causing it to bend, crack, and produce mountains, earthquakes, and volcanoes. Soil, water, coal, oil, gas and minerals that we use are found in the crust.

There are at least 90 chemical elements found in the crust. Only 5 of these elements make up about 92% of the crust's weight.

Beneath the crust is the mantle which extends to a depth of about 2900 kilometers or 1800 miles. It is made of a heavy solid rock called peridotite.

Beneath the mantle is the core. The core extends about 3500 kilometers or 2200 miles to the center of earth. The core is a mixture of about 90% iron and 10% nickel. The core has two parts. The outer core which is solid and the inner core which has a plastic form.

Great masses of hard material called rock makes up the solid part of the crust. Most of the rock on the surface is covered with soil. Rocks are divided into three main groups according to the way in which they were formed. The three kinds are: igneous, sedimentary, and metamorphic.

Igneous rocks are formed when magna below the earth's surface (crust) finds its way to the top and spills out. There are two types of igneous rocks: extrusive and intrusive.

Sedimentary rocks were formed from different sediments that accumulated for several thousand years and then were cemented together.

Metamorphic rocks are igneous and sedimentary rocks that were changed by heat and pressure.

Rocks are made up of one or more minerals. Minerals are chemical elements or compounds that are found naturally in the crust. They have an orderly arrangement of atoms and a definite crystal structure.

The last feature of the earth's surface is the ocean of air that surrounds earth called the atmosphere. The earth's surface has changed constantly since its origin and will continue to do so.

PRESENT-DAY KNOWLEDGE
OF
THE INSIDE OF THE EARTH

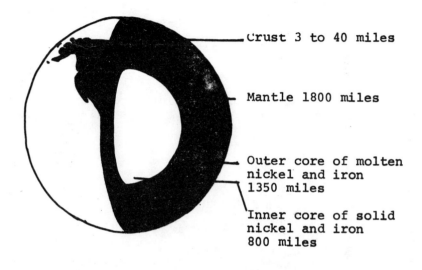

Crust 3 to 40 miles

Mantle 1800 miles

Outer core of molten
nickel and iron
1350 miles

Inner core of solid
nickel and iron
800 miles

Test your knowledge of competency 30.

1. The earth's crust is
    a. layers of rock
    b. the floors of the oceans
    c. the earth's continents
    d. a, b, and c

2. Which of the following is not a type of rock?
    a. igneous
    b. sedimentary
    c. morpheme
    d. metamorphic

3. Mountains, earthquakes, volcanoes, soil,
    water, coal, oil, gas, and minerals that we
    use are found in the
    a. earth's crust
    b. earth's mantle
    c. earth's core
    d. a, b, and c

4. Metamorphic rocks are
    a. igneous rocks changed by heat and pres-
        sure
    b. sedimentary rocks changed by heat and
        pressure
    c. igneous and sedimentary rocks changed by
        heat and pressure
    d. none of the above

Answers: 1. d, 2. c, 3. a, 4. c

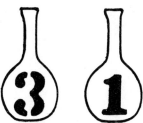

Competency 31:   Describe the effects of
natural processes (i.e., weathering, erosion,
deposition, earthquake, volcanoes) on the earth's
surface.

Weathering occurs whenever wind, water,
changes in temperature, and living things can act
on rock and other material.   There are two kinds
of weathering:

  1.   mechanical (or physical) weathering - the
       breaking down of rock into small pieces
       without any chemical changes in the rock
       itself.

  2.   chemical weathering - chemical changes
       take place in the rock, forming new
       products that can be carried away more
       easily than the original rock.

Weathering causes many changes in the earth.
Large peices of rock are broken down into smaller
and smaller pieces.   The remains of plants and
animals become mixed with the tiny pieces of
broken rock.   In this way, rock slowly becomes
part of the soil.

As rock near the top of mountains weathers
and falls, the height of those mountains becomes
lower.   Soil formed from the rock covers the lower
parts of the mountains and fills valleys.   Wind
and water carry some of the soil to other places.

As the layer of soil over the rock becomes
deeper, more plants are able to grow there.   Large

forests may eventually cover the land. Eventually, people may come to live in this region. The soil, formed from what was once rock, may then be used to grow food.

Erosion is the moving of soil, sand, and weathered rock from one place to another over the surface of the earth. As this material is moved, it rubs against and wears away other matter. For this reason, many scientists think of weathering as being part of the process of erosion.

By far the most important agent of erosion is running water. As water moves over the land, material carried by the water wears away rock and soil over which the water flows. It digs canyons, washes away dikes, and destroys homes.

Like running water, a glacier picks up rock fragments that act as tools in cutting its bed. Lakes and swamps are numerous in glaciated valleys, formed where the glaciers gouged basins in their channels or left piles of debris as dams.

Cutting of the shore by waves and removal of the debris by currents are responsible for the sometimes spectacular coastline scenery of the world.

Strong winds can carry large amounts of sand and soil long distances. Blowing sand slowly cuts away banks and carves interesting shapes out of rock.

Deposition is the depositing of materials caused by weathering and erosion. Most of the material transported by the agents of erosion is eventually deposited to form sediments of various sorts. The ultimate destination of erosional debris is the ocean, and the most widespread sediments accumulate in shallow parts of the ocean near continental margins.

Debris carried in time of flood is deposited

in gravel banks and sandbars when the swiftly flowing waters begin to recede. The flood plain of a meandering river is a site of deposition in occasional floods. Alluvial fans and deltas are formed by stream deposits.

The pile of debris around the end of the glacier, called a moraine, is left as a low ridge of hummocky topography when the glacier melts back.

Most important of the agents of deposition, since they handle by far the largest amount of sediment, are the currents of the seas and oceans. Visible deposits of waves and currents include beaches and sandbars, but the great bulk of the sediments brought to the ocean are laid down under water.

Wind piles sand grains on exposed beaches and in deserts into the low, shifting hills called dunes. Winds can turn large amounts of land into waste lands by removing the layer of soil necessary for plant growth or by dropping large amounts of materials on top of plants and killing them.

An earthquake, the most destructive of natural phenomena, consists of rapid vibrating motions of rock. The great majority of earthquakes originate within a few miles of the earth's surface, but some have been recorded which originated at depths as great as 700 kilometers. Earthquakes occur when faulting, and sometimes folding, takes place. These actions that cause earthquakes are also some of the causes for mountain formations.

Strong earthquakes can cause great rock slides, mud flows, and changes in stream beds. A river may be dammed up and a new lake produced.

Scientists have discovered that certain kinds of changes often take place before an earthquake. The water in wells often becomes muddy. The amount of radon, a gas, in the water may become greater. The ground above the fault may rise, sink, or become bent. Even animals often act differently just before an earthquake. Scientists are trying to find a way to predict earthquakes from observing such changes as these.

A volcano is formed by the cooling and hardening of hot, melted rock (lava). This lava is forced to the surface of the ground from a large pool deep in the earth.

When a volcano erupts, it can destroy many living things. The temperature of lava is about 1000°C (1,832°F). Living things cannot stand such a high temperature. Furthermore, many of the gases given off by volcanoes are poisonous to living things.

Where volcanoes have become extinct, in the recent geologic past, we find evidence of their former activity in isolated, cone-shaped mountains, in solidified lava flows, and in hot springs, geysers and steam vents. Many islands are really the tops of huge volcanic mountains that formed on the ocean floor.

Test your knowledge of competency 31.

1.   Most widespread sediments accumulate _____.
      a. in streams
      b. in the oceans
      c. on mountain tops
      d. in valleys

2.   Which of the following is not an agent of erosion?
      a. water
      b. ocean currents
      c. earthquakes
      d. wind

3. Which of the following is a volcano <u>least</u>
    likely to be responsible for?
    a. alluvial fans
    b. geysers
    c. islands
    d. lava flows

Answers: 1. b, 2. c, 3. a

****

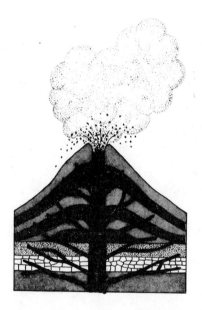

Hot liquid rock under pressure from the
earth's interior is pushed up to the surface
and gradually builds a volcanic mountain.

Competency 32-1: Identify the composition and general properties of seawater.

The composition of the seawater today is not the same as the water in the oceans long ago. At first the waters of the oceans were fresh, and they had no salts in them. As rain fell on the land, many minerals were dissolved and carried to the oceans by the rivers and streams. Each year the oceans become more and more salty.

Today, every 45 kilograms (100 lb.) of seawater contains about 1½ kilograms (3 1/3 lb.) of dissolved minerals. About three fourths of this mineral material is common salt, or sodium chloride. The rest of the minerals are salts of magnesium, calcium, and potassium.

Some of the dissolved minerals can be very valuable to man. Each cubic kilometer of seawater has one million tons of magnesium, which is used in planes and for other purposes, and almost all of the world's supply of magnesium is obtained from seawater. Bromine is also obtained from seawater, and it is used in making high-test gasoline and photographic film. Common salt, or sodium chloride, is obtained from seawater. Although a cubic kilometer of seawater has about fifty million dollars worth of gold in it, scientists say that it would cost more than fifty million dollars to recover this amount of gold.

Test your knowledge of competency 32-1.

1.   Of the mineral material found in seawater,
     about three fourths is
     a.   sodium chloride
     b.   calcium
     c.   magnesium
     d.   potassium

2.   Almost all the world's supply of which
     mineral is obtained from seawater?
     a.   bromine
     b.   salt
     c.   magnesium
     d.   calcium

3.   The composition of seawater has changed from
     what it was years ago because of what?
     a.   volcanic eruptions at the bottom of the
          ocean
     b.   the reaction of salt with decayed sea
          animals and plant life
     c.   rains dissolving and washing different
          minerals into the oceans
     d.   evaporation of the water

4.   Why is the gold in seawater not recovered by
     man?
     a.   There is not enough gold there to warrant
          this.
     b.   The expense of recovering the gold is
          greater than the value of the gold.
     c.   There is no known way to recover gold
          from the ocean.
     d.   Inflation has made gold worthless.

Answers: 1. a, 2. c, 3. c, 4. b

     Competency 32-2: Identify the composition
and general properties of seawater.

     The composition of seawater today is dif-
ferent than it was millions of years ago. The

ocean water at one time was fresh like inland rivers and lakes.

The minerals contained in the seawater today were gradually dissolved by the rains, and washed by the rivers and carried to the ocean.

The oceans become more and more salty every year. About 3.5 percent of seawater is salts. Every 45 kilograms (100 pounds) of seawater contains 1½ kilograms (3½ pounds) of dissolved minerals. Sodium chloride, or simple table salt, makes up about three fourths of these minerals.

Seawater also contains magnesium, sulfur, calcium, and potassium. The proportions of these elements in seawater are about the same throughout the world. The mixing action of waves and currents causes this sameness. In fact, the ocean contains all the elements that make up the minerals in the earth's crust.

The ocean also contains tons of precious minerals such as gold and silver. But the cost of removing these finely dissolved minerals would cost more than it would be worth.

Scientists have compared the composition of seawater with the composition of body fluids in man and animals. They have found that the proportion of the elements are much alike.

Test your knowledge of competency 32-2.

1. What mineral used in making planes is from seawater?
    a. magnesium
    b. sodium chloride
    c. gold
    d. potassium

2.   _____ causes the elements in seawater to remain much the same throughout the world.
   a. Rivers and streams
   b. Rains
   c. Waves and currents
   d. All of the above

3. Seawater contains
   a. sodium chloride
   b. magnesium and sulfur
   c. calcium and potassium
   d. all of the above

Answers: 1. a, 2. c, 3. d

Competency 33:   Identify career opportunities
in the sciences.

Career education has become a highly talked
about subject, because almost all children in
elementary classes today will spend a large amount
of their time as producers in the world of work.
This competency discusses some of the lines of
work in the field of science.

Children begin studying science in the
elementary school by learning the names of things.
They learn how things work through experiments.
These experiments and general ideas about science
allow the children to begin to build an understanding of science.

In high school, most students take a minimum
of one year of science. Students who plan to make
professional careers in pure and applied science
usually take at least two years of natural sciences.

College science courses are for the men and
women who plan to become professional scientists.
Even though most students are required to take
some science, the science major is required to
take three years of science courses.

A graduate student is more interested in
research or in a specific profession. Usually
after graduate school they go on the job training.

Science opportunities began many many years
ago. As far back as with the invention of the
wheel. Even though man may not have realized it,

this could have been the opening for many careers in the field of science.

Working in science can be one of the most rewarding careers a person can choose. Jobs are unlimited, because science holds such an important place in modern life.

Research: This is a field where a person works with knowledge that is fresh. He must know his field well and be acquainted with knowledge in related fields. Team research laboratories may have as many as twelve people working as a group on different aspects of the same problem.

Career opportunities have grown in scientific research and development. The physical sciences have the most critical need for scientists. The demand for biological scientists and social scientists are on the increase and are rapidly growing.

Teaching: There are more positions available for teaching science than there are teachers. Some of the positions include serving as a science consultant, teaching science in high school, teaching courses in college and graduate school.

Technicians: Technician jobs are increasing in industries and offices. They include medical technicians, dental assistants, laboratory assistants and computer operators. A supervising scientist usually directs their work. Though some college work is required for these positions, a major in science is not always needed.

In recent years many fields have opened in the line of science work. In the biological sciences some are:

1. Agronomy: This is the study of various soil and plant sciences to soil management and the raising of crops.

2. Anatomy: The study of the structures of a plant or animal, or of any of its parts.

3. Bacteriology: The study of bacteria, especially related to medicine and agriculture.

4. Biochemistry: The chemistry of biological substances and processes.

5. Biology: The science of life and life processes.

6. Biophysics: The physics of biological processes.

7. Botony: The biological science of plants.

8. Cytology: The branch of biology dealing with the study of the formation, structure and function of cells.

9. Ecology: The science of the relationships between organisms and their environments.

10. Embryology: The science dealing with the formation, early growth, and development of living organisms.

11. Genetics: The biology of heredity.

12. Histology: The anatomical study of the microscopic structure of animal and plant tissue.

13. Medicine: The science of diagnosing, treating, or preventing disease and other damage to the body or mind.

14. Morphology: The biological study of the form and structures of living organisms.

15. Pharmacology: The science of drugs,

including their composition, uses and
effects.

16. Paleontology: The study of fossils and
ancient life forms.

17. Physiology: The biological science of
essential and characteristic life processes, activities, and functions.

18. Taxonomy: The theory, principals, and
process of classifying organisms in
established categories and classification.

19. Zoology: The biological science of
animals.

In the physical sciences:

1. Acoustics: The science of sound.

2. Aerodynamics: The dynamics of gases,
especially of atmospheric interaction
with moving objects.

3. Astronomy: The scientific study of the
universe beyond the earth.

4. Chemistry: The science of the composition, structure, properties and reactions
of materials, especially of atoms and
molecular systems.

5. Chemurgy: The development of new
industrial chemical products from organic
raw materials, especially from those of
agricultural origin.

6. Dynamics: The study of the relationship
between motion and the forces affecting
motion.

7. Electro Chemistry: The science of interaction or inter conversion of electric

and chemical phenomena.

8. Electronics: The science and technology of electronic phenomena.

9. Engineering: The application of scientific principles to practical ends.

10. Geochemistry: The chemistry of the composition and alterations of the earth's crust.

11. Geology: The scientific study of the origin, history, and structure of the earth.

12. Geophysics: The physics of geological phenomena, including meteorology, oceanography, gradsey, and serismology.

13. Metallurgy: The science or procedures of extracting metals from their ores, of purifying metals and of creating useful objects from metals.

14. Meteorology: The science dealing with the phenomena of the atmosphere, especially weather and weather conditions.

15. Micro Chemistry: Chemistry that deals with minute quantities of materials, weighing one milligram or less.

16. Nuclear Physics: The scientific study of the forces, reactions and internal structures of atomic nuclei.

17. Optics: The scientific study of light and vision.

18. Physical Chemistry: The scientific analysis of the properties and behavior of chemical systems primarily by physical theory and technique.

19. Physics: Science of matter and energy and of interactions between the two grouped in traditional fields.

20. Solid State Physics: Characteristics of or pertaining to the physical properties of solid materials, especially to electromagnetic, thermodynamic, and properties of crystalline solids.

21. Statics: The equilibrium mechanics of stationary bodies.

22. Thermodynamics: The physics of the relationship between heat and other forms of energy.

Test your knowledge of competency 33.

1. Career education has become more of a concern in the last few years because
   a. it is a new field of science
   b. it provides opportunities for children
   c. children will spend a large amount of their time as producers of the world
   d. children will spend a large amount of their time taking career education courses in school

2. Working in science can be a rewarding career because
   a. it is very easy work and not much preparation is needed
   b. jobs are unlimited and science holds an important place in modern life
   c. no college credit is required
   d. science holds an important place in modern life and jobs are limited

3. In recent years many fields have opened up in the sciences, some are
   a. agronomy, biochemistry, and reading
   b. genetics, histrology, medicine
   c. paleontology, painting, pharmacology
   d. solid state physics, statics, sewing

Answers: 1. c, 2. b, 3. b

****

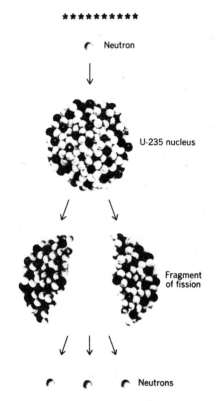

Neutron

U-235 nucleus

Fragment of fission

Neutrons

When the nucleus of a uranium-235 atom is split by a neutron, a vast amount of energy is released, as well as neutron "bullets" to split more U-235 atoms. This is fission. In fussion even more energy is released.

Test 1
Test Your Knowledge

DIRECTIONS: In front of each numeral write the
letter which represents the best
answer for each item.

1. The major contribution of the nature study
    movement was that it
    a. encourages teachers to read nature books
        to children.
    b. directed attention to the need for teach-
        ing science in elementary schools.
    c. prepared teachers to teach science in
        elementary school.
    d. helped develop a curriculum for elemen-
        tary science.

2. An example of a functional skill is
    a. problem solving.
    b. creative thinking.
    c. deduction.
    d. measuring.

3. Jerome S. Bruner's theory of learning was
    basically concerned with
    a. four development stages: sensori-motor,
        preoperational, concrete operations, and
        formal operations.
    b. teaching and learning of inquiry.
    c. four levels of science instruction:
        elementary, sixth and seventh grade,
        eleventh grade, third year of college.
    d. learning can be effective for any child
        in some form at any stage of development.

4. Functional skills are those involving
    a. observing and problem solving.
    b. critical and creative thinking, induction,
        deduction, and measuring.
    c. describing, manipulating, recording,
        measuring, and observing.
    d. inference, manipulating, deduction, and
        problem solving.

5. Which of the following would be the best science curriculum?
   a. a curriculum project developed at a major university
   b. an elementary science program developed by the school system designed to meet the needs of the students
   c. a plan based only on incidents in the classroom
   d. none of these

6. Oral reports given by students should last
   a. about fifteen minutes.
   b. about an hour.
   c. about thirty minutes.
   d. about five minutes.

7. If you had a choice of the following activities, which would you choose as an initiating activity?
   a. a thought provoking demonstration
   b. film
   c. field trip
   d. speaker

8. A science program should have scope and sequence. The science program should
   a. be broad in scope.
   b. give children ample opportunity to learn major concepts.
   c. be drawn from all areas of science.
   d. begin as early as kindergarten
   e. a, b, and d only.
   f. a, b, c, and d.

9. The scope and sequence in the Science curriculum refers to
   a. content.
   b. correlation.
   c. grade level.
   d. all of the above.
   e. a and c.

10. A science demonstration serves as a
    a. way of illustration.
    b. teacher of procedure.
    c. reinforcer.
    d. way of teaching a concept.
    e. all of the above.

11. Objectives for teachers in a Science Unit
    should be
    a. to teach science vocabulary.
    b. to teach content of science.
    c. to teach content and process of science.
    d. to teach process of science.

12. The well-planned elementary school science
    program should have
    a. a large quantity of complicated, expen-
       sive equipment.
    b. only simple material since science in
       elementary school should be kept simple.
    c. a variety of materials easily accessible
       to teachers and students including both
       simple and complex materials.
    d. a few simple materials because most
       teachers know little about science and
       are unfamiliar with science materials or
       equipment.

13. Oral methods of evaluation are especially
    necessary in which elementary grades?
    a. lower elementary grades
    b. middle elementary grades
    c. upper elementary grades
    d. all of the above

14. The most structured of all the different
    kinds of units currently in use are
    a. resource units.
    b. teaching units.
    c. textbook units.
    d. curriculum project units.

15. To ensure provision for individual dif-
    ferences, the teacher should plan activities
    for the
    a. slow learner.
    b. average learner.
    c. fast learner.
    d. all of the above.

16. Science kits are especially useful when
    a. the teacher has a weak background in
       science.
    b. the administrator would like to encourage
       teachers to conduct science learning in
       the classroom.
    c. the school does not have a structured
       science program.
    d. all of the above.

17. The greatest of all forces that produce ero-
    sion is
    a. ice.
    b. water.
    c. wind.
    d. sun.

18. The earth is made up of three separate layers:
    the crust, the mantle, and the core. Which
    of the following is NOT true?
    a. Geologists have found that the tempera-
       ture rises as they go deeper into the
       earth's crust.
    b. In the earth's mantle are found the coal,
       oil, gas and minerals that we use.
    c. The crust is thickest underneath the
       continents.
    d. The presence of metals in the core seems
       to confirm the theory that, as the earth
       cooled the heavier materials settled
       toward the center, and the lighter
       materials floated toward the surface.

19. All of the following statements are true about the moon except one statement. Which statement is not true?
    a. The moon travels around the earth in an orbit.
    b. The moon revolves around the earth in a clockwise direction.
    c. The moon revolves around the earth in the same direction as the earth revolves around the sun.
    d. The moon has about 2 weeks of daylight followed by 2 weeks of nighttime.

20. The Cenozoic era which began about 60 million years ago, and has lasted until today is also known as
    a. the age of fish.
    b. the age of reptiles.
    c. the age of mammals.
    d. the age of amphibians.

21. There are three kinds of rocks--igeneous sedimentary, and metamorphic. The following is true.
    a. igeneous rocks are formed from molten materials below the earth's crust
    b. sedimentary rocks are found only in beds of streams, lakes, and oceans where the material has settled to the bottom
    c. metamorphic rocks are found only around volcanoes
    d. all of the above

22. Which of the following best describes the effects of the sun on the Earth?
    a. The sun causes the year on the earth.
    b. The sun revolves in an elliptical path around the earth.
    c. The sun causes day and night.
    d. a, c, and e.
    e. The sun causes the seasons and the weather on the earth, and serves as a source of energy for the earth.

23. The solid part of the earth's crust is made up of hard masses of material called
    a. moho.
    b. minerals.
    c. rock.
    d. streak plate.

24. Find the statement below which is correct about the earth's layers.
    a. Beneath the earth's crust is the core, or middle layer.
    b. The crust is the thickest layer of the earth, which is mostly granite and basalt.
    c. The core is composed of two parts: the outer and the inner core.
    d. There is a boundary or zone, commonly called the Moho, between the mantle and the core.

25. All seeds have a(an)
    a. seed coat.
    b. stored food.
    c. embryo.
    d. all of the above.

26. Mammals are members of the animal phylum called
    a. Arthropods.
    b. Echinoderms.
    c. Annelids.
    d. Chordata.

27. The _____, a strong sheet of muscle between the chest and the abdomen, plays an important part in breathing.
    a. Epiglottis
    b. windpipe
    c. pharynx
    d. diaphragm

28. The normal temperature of an adult's blood is about _____° Fahrenheit.
    a. 96.4
    b. 98.6
    c. 93.8
    d. 95.7

29. Which of the following is not a main part of a flowering seed plant?
    a. roots
    b. bulbs
    c. stems
    d. leaves
    e. flowers

30. All of the following are forms of reproduction except
    a. fission.
    b. symbiosis.
    c. conjugation.
    d. budding.

31. The upper level of ground water in the soaked soil and rock is called the water table. Which of the following is true?
    a. The level of the water table follows the general contour of the land.
    b. A spring is formed when the water table meets the earth's surface.
    c. The height of the water table depends on how much ran has fallen recently.
    d. All of the above.

32. Oceanographers use many devices and instruments to study the ocean. Which of the following is not a device used by oceanographers?
    a. deep sea camera
    b. sonic depth recorder
    c. water sampling bottle
    d. barometer

33. Select the statement about the moon which is not true.
    a. The moon has no atmosphere.
    b. The temperature on the surface of the moon is always between 70°F and 75°F.
    c. The moon is a very large ball of rocky material that revolves around the earth.
    d. The moon has no water or water vapor.

34. The speed (25,000m/h) at which an object must reach when leaving the earth's surface to overcome the force of gravity is known as
    a. the force of acceleration.
    b. escape velocity.
    c. overpowering thrust.
    d. orbital force.

35. Oxygen and nitrogen make up what percent of our air?
    a. 75%
    b. 50%
    c. 37%
    d. 99%
    e. 7%

36. The exosphere is _____.
    a. the lowest layer of the atmosphere
    b. the layer above the troposphere
    c. the layer of the atmosphere with almost no air at all
    d. the layer of the atmosphere with a special form of oxygen, called ozone

37. All the substances that make up matter can be divided into three main classes, which are
    a. chemical, natural, mineral
    b. nuclear, atomic, hydrogenic
    c. elements, compounds, mixtures
    d. positive, negative, neutral

38. For burning to take place what three things are needed?
    a. fuel, heat, air
    b. heat, gas, air
    c. fuel, oxygen, heat
    d. oxygen, carbon, nitrogen

39. The passing along heat by radian energy waves is called _____.
    a. conduction
    b. radiation
    c. convection
    d. insulation

40. A hot air balloon rises because
    a. as the air is heated the molecules move faster and force the balloon off the ground.
    b. the hot air in the balloon is lighter than the air surrounding it which causes the balloon to rise.
    c. the hot air molecules become electrically charged and are pulled away from the earth.
    d. of the physical and chemical changes taking place in the air.

41. Which of the following statements best describes temperature?
    a. Temperature has to do with the degree of "hotness" or "coldness" of a material.
    b. Temperature depends upon the speed that the molecules in a material are moving.
    c. a and b
    d. Temperature has to do only with the amount of heat a material has.

42. This is the first class lever (the fulcrum is anywhere between the effort and the resistance). Which of these statements is true of a first class lever?

effort · resistance

$$\frac{\qquad\qquad O \qquad\qquad}{}$$

fulcrum

a. It does not change the direction of the force.
b. A nutcracker is a first class lever.
c. The effort pushes in one direction and the resistance moves in the opposite direction.
d. None of these.

43. Sounds travel through
a. solids, liquids and gases.
b. pitch, intensity and quality.
c. frequency, decibels, overtones.
d. vacuums.

44. Light, smooth objects
a. absorb more light than they reflect.
b. reflect more light than they absorb.
c. absorb and reflect equal amounts of light.
d. do not reflect any light.

45. A black material appears black because
a. when light strikes a material all colored lights are absorbed except red.
b. all the colored lights are absorbed so that not one light is reflected to the eye.
c. black is the absence of all colors.
d. black is the presence of all colors-- except white.

46. The unit of electrical pressure that is a
    measure of force pushing the electron through
    a conductor and overcoming the resistance of
    the conductor is
    a. a volt.
    b. an ohm.
    c. an ampere.
    d. a watt.

47. What form of energy uses the generator and
    the piezoelectric cell?
    a. chemical
    b. light
    c. heat
    d. mechanical

48. The higher sound will be made by
    a. a tight thin rubber band.
    b. a wide thick rubber band.
    c. they will both be the same.
    d. neither will make a high sound.

49. All of the statements apply to work except
    a. Because of friction, the amount of work
        put out by a machine is less than the
        work put into a machine.
    b. No machine can produce more work than the
        work that was put into the machine.
    c. The speed with which the effort or
        resistance moves will make no difference
        in the amount of work done.
    d. No matter how much effort or resistance
        is exerted, if they have not moved
        through a distance work has been done.

50. Which of the following is not an example of
    an organ in a mammal?
    a. heart
    b. liver
    c. brain
    d. none of the above

51. Blood is described as
    a. liquid tissue.
    b. mostly water
    c. containing salts.
    d. all of the above.

52. The method of splitting nuclei of atoms is
    a. fusion.
    b. fission.
    c. deacceleration.
    d. climation.

53. The force required to keep an object sliding
    compared to the force required to start an
    object sliding is
    a. less.
    b. more.
    c. about the same.

54. The method of heat travel, where energy is
    passed along from molecule to molecule by
    bumping or collision, is called
    a. convection.
    b. secretion.
    c. illumination.
    d. conduction.

55. A method of heat travel that takes place only
    in gases and liquids which are called fluids
    is called
    a. conduction.
    b. convection.
    c. radiation.
    d. none of the above.

56. Sound is a form of
    a. vibration.
    b. motion.
    c. energy.
    d. percussion.

57. Shadows are formed when the following material is placed in the path of rays of light
a. transparent
b. opaque
c. translucent
d. darkened

58. The law of magnetic attraction states
a. two unlike poles attract each other.
b. two like poles repel each other.
c. both a and b.
d. neither a nor b.

59. What is the main reason that seeds do not need sunlight when they first begin to grow?
a. All green plants do not make use of the process of photosynthesis.
b. At first the seeds live off the stored food while they are still in the ground.
c. The seed coat covering the seed cannot be broken.
d. The embryo inside the seed has not yet come alive.

60. The apparent nightly motion of the stars is due to
a. the turning of the earth.
b. the motion of everything in the universe.
c. the stars in the milky way.
d. all of the above.

61. Earthquakes often occur along lines called
a. vertical lines.
b. diagonal lines.
c. fault lines.
d. none of the above.

62. Since gravity decreases with distance the force required to maintain a satellite in orbit
a. decreases with distance from the earth.
b. increases with distance from the earth.
c. remains the same.
d. none of the above

63. The circulatory system has the following function(s).
    a. It carries digested food to the cells in the body.
    b. It brings oxygen to the cells for burning.
    c. It takes away the waste materials produced by the cells and carries these materials to organs that remove them from the body.
    d. all of the above.

64. Scientists have discovered that all atoms are made up of three smaller kinds of particles
    a. electrons
    b. protons
    c. neutrons
    d. molecules
    e. a, b, and c

65. The chemical reaction, which takes place when a material combines with oxygen is
    a. oxidation.
    b. combustion.
    c. oxygen dioxide.
    d. explosion.

Test II
Test Your Knowledge

DIRECTIONS: In front of each numeral write the letter which represents the best answer for each item.

1. From the following list choose the most important characteristic of a child that would help him in science.
   a. his age
   b. his sex
   c. his curiosity
   d. his size

2. The major objectives for elementary science are to help children best in which of the following ways?
   a. learning concepts
   b. learning key operations
   c. developing problem solving and critical thinking skills
   d. developing behavioral outcomes such as scientific skills, attitudes, interests, and appreciation
   e. all of the above

3. The psychologist who developed a theory of intellectual development in children was
   a. Robert M. Gagne.
   b. Marilyn R. Mazer.
   c. Jean Piaget.
   d. Jerome S. Bruner.
   e. George Spache.

4. Which one of the following had the biggest impact on the U.S. becoming concerned about its serious shortage of scientific manpower?
   a. When Russia threatened the U.S.
   b. When the U.S. government realized that nature study was not successful in the schools.
   c. When the NSSE published its yearbook concerning the problems of science education.
   d. When Sputnik was sent into orbit.

213

5. When children learn the process of science they
   a. gain insight and practice in the different methods that scientists use to solve problems.
   b. become familiar with effective ways of working.
   c. acquire experience in thinking critically and creatively.
   d. a and c.
   e. a, b, and c.

6. Which of the following statements is true?
   a. Open-ended experiments is the only way to insure that learning will take place.
   b. The teacher should teach whatever she wants without carefully planning and selecting the science content.
   c. Learning facts in science is not important at all.
   d. When children learn science content, they should use an inquiry and discovery approach to insure learning not memorization.

7. Science programs should meet one of the following prerequisites.
   a. Science programs should be concerned with key concepts and how science helps us in our daily life.
   b. Science learning should be organized only around incidents that occur in the classroom.
   c. The science program should not be coordinated with other parts of the K-12 program.
   d. Concepts should be above the child's level of maturity and comprehension to challenge him.

8. An effective way of using a field trip with students who have little or not background in the topic to be studied is to
   a. allow the pupils to participate in the planning of the trip.
   b. use the field trip to introduce a unit and create interest.
   c. use the field trip while the class is in the middle of a unit to answer their questions.
   d. invite a resource person to the classroom.

9. A well-developed science program
   a. insures that the program will be a successful one.
   b. will make a large difference in the amount and kind of science being taught and learned in the elementary school.
   c. does not affect the success or failure of the program.
   d. none of the above.

10. The methods of teaching science are the means whereby the children use inquiry and discovery to learn
    a. the content of science.
    b. the process of science.
    c. a and b.
    d. none of the above.

11. When planning and constructing the units the teacher or curriculum committee does all except
    a. select the objectives.
    b. develop the means for arousing pupil interest.
    c. provide for the necessary laboratory materials.
    d. does not allow for individual differences.

12. When selecting science content for an elementary science program, one should _____.
    a. select content that will provide an understanding of other communities rather than the familiar community in which they live
    b. choose a program of science within itself, not correlating with the rest of the curriculum
    c. research on mental, emotional, and physical behavior of children
    d. not include the area of living things, for it is not important

13. Which one of the following statements is true about experiments and demonstrations?
    a. Children should be exposed only to the "why" and "what" of science rather than the "how much" of science.
    b. All numerous and complex concepts involved with the experiments of demonstrations should be learned the first time, for they can't be repeated.
    c. The real value gained in experiments or demonstrations helps answer questions about things that are happening in the child's daily environment.

14. A teaching unit differs from a resource unit in that _____.
    a. it contains only the objectives, activities, materials and bibliography that will be used in a unit
    b. it contains many more objectives, activities, materials, and bibliographys that will be used in the unit
    c. the teacher selects the concept to be learned
    d. the teacher organizes concepts into a logical learning sequence

15. The field trip can be effective as a teaching technique only when it has
    a. very brief preliminary investigation and planning.
    b. a purpose.
    c. a small group of children involved.
    d. been planned by children.

16. Which one of the following is generally considered the most valid type of objective test item?
    a. true-false
    b. completion
    c. multiple-choice
    d. matching

17. If the evaluation you use is effective it should
    a. appraise achievement.
    b. identify children's strength and weaknesses.
    c. pre-test.
    d. plan for future instruction.
    e. determine effectiveness of teaching method.
    f. a - e.

18. Which of the following is true of an effective and successful evaluation of a science program?
    a. Teachers should evaluate toward the end of a unit.
    b. Reliability is the degree with which a technique measures what it intends to measure.
    c. The objectives to be evaluated will play an important part on the kind of instrument selected.
    d. The question-and-answer method is widely used in the elementary grades and has a high reliability.

19. Advantages in using objective test evaluation procedures are
    a. they can be scored very objectively.
    b. they tend to have high validity and reliability.
    c. they can be designed to evaluate outcomes.
    d. all of the above.

20. Teachers have experienced some difficulties in teaching the units developed by the elementary science curriculum projects because
    a. b and d.
    b. some teachers are unfamiliar with the inquiry and discovery approach.
    c. the units were poorly written.
    d. some teachers are unfamiliar with the wide variety of materials and have an inadequate science background.
    e. b, c, and d.

21. Until recently scientists measured vast distances in the universe by using a measurement called a light year. They now use a parsec which is
    a. 7 light years.
    b. 6½ light years.
    c. 2 light years.
    d. 3½ light years.

22. The theory that proposes that the sun and planets were formed from a large, whirling cloud of hot gas and dust is known as
    a. the dust cloud theory.
    b. the exploding star theory.
    c. the planetismal theory.
    d. the nebular theory.

23. Between Mars and Jupiter there is a belt of several thousand bodies of different sizes called
    a. fireballs.
    b. asteroids.
    c. meteors.
    d. comets.

24. The roots are the part of the plant that
_____.
   a. do not need water
   b. grow downward into the ground
   c. need no seed to begin to grow
   d. have a tip at the root called a cotyledon, which protects the delicate end of the root

25. Stems may be found _____.
   a. above the ground
   b. below the ground
   c. both above and below the ground
   d. all of the above

26. Which of the following is not a characteristic shared by all vertebrates?
   a. They have backbones.
   b. They are warm-blooded.
   c. Their skeletons are inside their bodies.
   d. They usually have two pairs of limbs, or appendages attached to their bodies at the shoulder and hip.

27. The necessary food materials the body needs can be divided into which of the following classes?
   a. proteins, carbohydrates, minerals
   b. vitamins, minerals, proteins, carbohydrates
   c. carbohydrates, fats, proteins, minerals, vitamins, and water
   d. carbohydrates, proteins, minerals, vitamins, and water

28. If a person has symptoms such as loss of appetite, poor digestion, headache, tiredness or irratiability, he may be suffering from a lack of which vitamin?
   a. vitamin B
   b. vitamin C
   c. vitamin P-P
   d. vitamin K

29. Which of the following is true of animals?
    a. Reptiles are part of the special group called vertebrate.
    b. Birds are so active that they need large amounts of food, and they seem to be eating all the time.
    c. All mammals have lungs for breathing.
    d. All of the above.

30. A fat person floats more easily than a thin person because
    a. fat people are usually more agile.
    b. a fat person resists gravity more easily.
    c. a skinny person is too thin.
    d. a fat person displaces more water.
    e. a fat person weighs more.

31. Condensation takes place because
    a. there is a change in molecular motion of the molecules of water vapor in the air.
    b. a and c.
    c. air contracts when cooled.
    d. air expands when cooled.

32. Select the statement about the water table which is not true.
    a. During dry weather the level of the water table sinks, and during rainy weather the level rises.
    b. As a rule, the level of the water table follows the general contours of the land, sloping where the surface of the land slopes, and rising where the surface rises.
    c. The lower level of the ground water is the soaked soil and rock is called the water table.
    d. The ground water can flow through a porous layer of soil and rock, and thus makes it possible for water to enter the ground at one place and to appear in another place later.

220

33. Which of the following is not true of
    tornadoes?
    a. Tornadoes usually occur in the afternoon.
    b. Tornadoes are most frequent during the
        late summer and fall.
    c. Tornadoes may occur in any level land
        area.
    d. Tornadoes are usually accompanied by
        lightning, thunder, and heavy rain.

34. An instrument used to measure relative
    humidity is
    a. a barometer.
    b. an anemometer.
    c. a rain gauge.
    d. a hygrometer.

35. In the northern hemisphere, there is a narrow
    band of high speed winds called
    a. trade winds.
    b. jet stream.
    c. a monsoon.
    d. prevailing westerlies.

36. When water vapor changes into a liquid, the
    change is called
    a. respiration.
    b. precipitation.
    c. evaporation.
    d. condensation.

37. Which is not true when dealing with mass?
    a. Mass helps the earth force of gravity.
    b. A body will have the same mass, whether
        it is on the earth's surface or far out
        into space.
    c. Mass has nothing to do with the earth's
        pull of gravity.

38. The Law of Conservation of matter and energy does not state
    a. neither matter nor energy can be destroyed, but either can be changed into other forms of matter or energy.
    b. matter can be changed into energy, but energy can not be changed into matter.
    c. the total amount of matter and energy in the universe always stays the same.

39. Which of the following is a method of heat travel that takes place only in gases and liquids?
    a. radiation
    b. convection
    c. conduction
    d. none of these

40. Which of the following is true of machines?
    a. The longer an inclined plane, the more force that is needed to move a body up the incline.
    b. A pully is a wheel that turns with a movable axle.
    c. In using levers, the fulcrum, effort, and resistance always have the same position.
    d. There is much friction between a wedge and the object; therefore friction is helpful in that it keeps the wedge from slipping out.

41. The steam engine is called an external combustion machine because
    a. the fuel is burned outside the engine.
    b. water turbines are used to run the generators to produce power.
    c. the many water blades made the water produce the power.
    d. the blades in the boiler are set at an angle and slope backward so that the produced steam will be the maximum power.

42. A screw is a type of
   a. wedge.
   b. lever.
   c. inclined plane.
   d. pulley.

43. Magnets can be made to loose their magnetism by
   a. dropping or striking them.
   b. a, c, and d.
   c. placing the north-seeking poles of two magnets side by side or on top of each other.
   d. heating them.
   e. placing the south-seeking poles of two magnets side by side.

44. Light is a form of energy. Which of the following is true?
   a. Electromagnetic waves with long wavelengths have a high frequency.
   b. Mirrors that curve inward are convex mirrors and bring rays of light together.
   c. Some parts of the shadow are darker than other parts.
   d. Light rays travel in a straight line, therefore light cannot travel in different directions.

45. Sound travels _____ .
   a. faster and better in lighter gases, when the molecules are further apart
   b. faster and better through gases than liquids
   c. faster and better through hard solids than through gases or liquids
   d. in a vacuum, where there are no molecules to carry the sound waves

46. The vocal cords are _____ .
   a. stretched over the top of the voice box
   b. two thin but strong bands of tissue
   c. higher in pitch when tighter
   d. all of the above

223

47. Sound travels through the air at the rate of about
    a. 2,100 feet a second.
    b. 1,100 feet a second.
    c. 1,582 feet per second.
    d. 1,000 feet a second.

48. Of the following statements concerning heat, which is not true?
    a. If we add enough heat energy to a solid, the solid becomes a liquid.
    b. If we take enough heat energy away from a liquid, the liquid becomes a solid.
    c. If we add enough heat energy to a liquid, it becomes a gas.
    d. If we take enough heat energy away from a gas, the gas becomes a liquid.
    e. none of the above

49. Applying the definition of friction, "the force that resists the movement of one material over another material", which of the following statements is not true?
    a. The amount of area between two surfaces does not affect friction.
    b. The nature of the surface affects friction.
    c. Sliding friction is less than starting friction.
    d. Rolling friction is more than sliding friction.

50. According to the Law of Conservation of Matter and Energy, which of the following is true?
    a. Neither matter nor energy can be destroyed, but either can be changed into other forms of matter or energy.
    b. Matter can be changed into energy, and energy can be changed into matter.
    c. both a and b
    d. neither a nor b

51. Which of the following is the main organ for digesting food in the human body?
    a. mouth
    b. esophagus
    c. stomach
    d. small intestine
    e. large intestine

52. Which of the following animals are not considered to be cold-blooded?
    a. birds
    b. fish
    c. amphibians
    d. reptiles

53. The three characteristics of sound are
    a. pitch, frequency, and quality.
    b. resonance, pitch, and percussion.
    c. pitch, intensity, and quality.
    d. all of the above.

54. The primary colors are
    a. red, yellow, and blue.
    b. green, blue, and red.
    c. blue, red, and yellow.
    d. none of the above.

55. Electricity is a flow of
    a. atoms.
    b. neutrons.
    c. protons.
    d. electrons.

56. The space where the molecules are pressed closer together is called
    a. compression.
    b. deinclination.
    c. submergence.
    d. depression.

57. The speed of light is approximately
    a. 186,000 miles per second.
    b. 6 trillion miles per second.
    c. twice as fast as the speed of sound.
    d. none of the above.

58. An electromagnet can be made stronger by
    a. increasing the number of turns of wire
        around the core.
    b. decreasing the number of turns of wire
        around the core.
    c. using alternating current (AC) instead of
        direct current (DC).
    d. none of the above.

59. Materials that will allow electrons to travel
    through them are called
    a. nonisolaters.
    b. conductors.
    c. insulators.
    d. plastics.

60. The statement that would be considered the
    more correct is
    a. Our universe is one of many galaxies.
    b. The sun and the solar system are parts of
        a galaxy called the GALAXY.
    c. The milky way is the part of our solar
        system that is made up of a group of
        satellites called planets, asteroids,
        comets, meteors.
    d. all of the above statements.
    e. none of the above statements.

61. When a sizable layer of air next to the
    earth's surface is cooled below its dewpoint
    the water vapor in this layer condenses into
    tiny water droplets to form
    a. hail.
    b. drizzle.
    c. fog.
    d. snow.

62. Any heavenly body revolving around a planet
    is called a
    a. moon.
    b. satellite.
    c. sputnik.
    d. star.

63. The common element(s) in all planets
    a. all revolve counterclockwise.
    b. all contain the same basic chemicals.
    c. all obtain energy from the sun.
    d. all rotate on an axis.
    e. a, b, c, and d.

64. Which statement is untrue about the body's
    sensory nerve endings?
    a. Nerve endings sensitive to touch are very
        near the surface of skin.
    b. Each nerve ending can produce only one
        sensation.
    c. Nerve endings sensitive to pressure are
        located deeper in the skin.
    d. Sensory nerve endings are spread out
        evenly over the skin.

65. Which makes it possible for molecules to come
    together and form the three physical states
    of matter?
    a. cohesion
    b. inertia
    c. spasticity
    d. adhesion

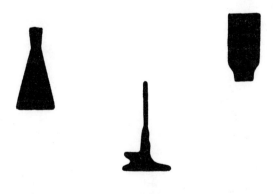

Answers to Tests

	Test I	Test II		Test I	Test II
1.	b	c	34.	b	d
2.	d	e	35.	d	b
3.	d	c	36.	c	d
4.	c	d	37.	c	a
5.	b	e	38.	c	b
6.	d	d	39.	b	b
7.	a	a	40.	b	d
8.	f	b	41.	c	a
9.	e	b	42.	c	c
10.	e	c	43.	a	b
11.	c	d	44.	b	c
12.	c	c	45.	b	c
13.	a	c	46.	a	d
14.	b	a	47.	d	b
15.	d	b	48.	a	e
16.	d	c	49.	d	d
17.	b	f	50.	d	c
18.	b	c	51.	d	d
19.	b	d	52.	b	a
20.	c	a	53.	a	c
21.	a	d	54.	d	b
22.	e	d	55.	b	d
23.	c	b	56.	c	a
24.	c	b	57.	b	a
25.	d	d	58.	c	a
26.	d	b	59.	b	b
27.	d	c	60.	a	b
28.	b	b	61.	c	c
29.	b	d	62.	a	b
30.	b	d	63.	d	e
31.	d	b	64.	e	d
32.	d	c	65.	a	a
33.	b	b			

Index

Air, 81
  human influences
    on, 81
Air masses, 162-171
  fronts, 164,167
  storms, 169
Alcohol, 51-53
Atoms, 85, 90
Authority, 8

Biomes, 46

Cells, 12-17
  animal, 15, 16,
    25, 28
  function of, 17-21
  main parts, 13
  plant, 15, 22,
    23, 24
  structure of,
    17-21
Chain, food, 42
Climate, 175
  fauna, 177
  flora, 175,176
Community safety,
  75-78

Disease, communicable,
  48-50
Drugs, 50, 51

Earth, 153-155, 179-182
  size and shape to its
    rotation and revolu-
    tion, 153-155
  structure, 179-182
Energy, 105, 106
  chemical, 105
  electrical, 105
  heat, 105
  light, 106

mechanical, 105
nuclear, 105
solar, 106
Experimentation, 1-3

Fluids and solids,
  109-131
  air circulation,
    118, 119
  astrophysics,
    110, 111
  blood, 123-127
  fluid mechanics,
    109,110
  heat, 118
  oscillations, 114
  stability, 111
  thermal convection,
    118
  tides, 114
  urinary drop
    spectrometer,
    127-131
  viscosity, 117,118
  waves in, 113

Heat, 132-135
  general character-
    istics, 132-135
Home safety, 71-75
Human health problems,
  48-57
  alcohol, 51-53
  communicable disease,
    48-50
  drugs, 50,51
  tobacco, 54,55
Human influences on,
  79-82
  air, 81
  natural systems,
    79-82

Index

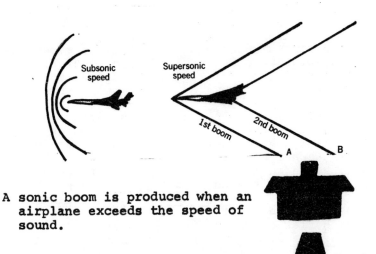

A sonic boom is produced when an
airplane exceeds the speed of
sound.

ABOUT THE AUTHOR

Dr. Mary Oellerich Dalnoki Miklos has taught at all levels of education: elementary, junior high, senior high, and college.

Among honors received while attending high school are: highest mark in American history, second highest academic average, only graduate to have exempted all exams for four years (minimum average 90), only graduate to have a perfect attendance record for four years. Among college honors are: graduated cum laude, one of three women selected in the U.S. to receive an academic scholarship based on merit awarded by Alpha Delta Kappa. November 1977 she received the GOLD APPLE AWARD in Education presented by the Florida Publishing Company's EVE Awards for the greatest contribution to education in the Jacksonville, Florida area. January 1, 1981 the Officers and Board of Trustees enrolled Dr. Miklos as a member of the National Geographic Society in recognition of her support of this nonprofit scientific and educational organization chartered in 1888 for diffusing geographic knowledge and promoting research and exploration. She has received numerous awards from student groups for service to and leadership in education.

Publications include over 200 articles dealing with the teaching of mathematics and science (K-12), curriculum development, student council, competency based teacher education, and an international publication entitled "Understanding through Knowledge". Books include Student of Teaching as Decision Maker, Student Teacher as Decision Maker, Preparation for Criterion-Referenced Tests: A Brief Review of Mathematical Competencies for Teachers of Early Childhood, Mathematical Ideas, Preparation for Criterion-Referenced Tests: A Brief Review of Scientific Competencies for Teachers of Early Childhood, Preparation for Criterion-Referenced Tests: A Brief Review of Mathematics Competencies for Teachers of Middle

Grades, and this one, Preparation for Criterion-Referenced Tests: A Brief Review of Scientific Competencies for Teachers of Middle Grades. Other books are in the planning stage.